Praise for

Character Education through Stories, Music, and Imagery

Linda received a Be Inspired Grant from the Tryon Fine Arts Council, NC, to bring *Character Education through Stories, Music, and Imagery* to each classroom. Linda shared with my class. It was very beneficial for the children, and they enjoyed it.

One of the most important lessons taught in kindergarten is living in community. Linda Powell's class on honesty taught with story, reflective time, and music at an age-appropriate level helped them to understand the concept as well as the importance of honesty.

Julie Maziarka
Kindergarten teacher
Sunny View Elementary School

The transition from story and relaxation technique can help children to explore, dare to fight in unknown situations, or provide a chance to meet something they love again.

Shanaree Laohapongphan, PhD
Private therapist / School counselor

Linda is gifted in being able to teach kids about tapping into the heart through her gentle, fun, and original stories.

As a parent of two school-age kids, I struggle to find resources that complement and support what we have made a priority to teach our kids. They have great teachers in school for academics, but there is a gap in teaching the core of being integrated, whole, and contributing in a positive way. Linda's book helps fill that gap and supports the kids to remember what is really important in life, a connection with our hearts.

Connie Baglia, RN
Mother of two bright spirited kids

Character Education
through
Stories, Music, and Imagery

Linda T. Powell

ASHEVILLE, NORTH CAROLINA

Copyright © 2023 by Linda T. Powell

All rights reserved. No part of this book shall be reproduced or transmitted in any form or by any means, electronic, mechanical, magnetic, photographic including photocopying, recording, or by an information storage and retrieval system, without prior written permission of the publisher. No patent liability is assumed with respect to the use of the information contained herein. Although every precaution has been taken in the preparation of this book, the publisher and author assume no responsibility for errors or omissions. Neither is any liability assumed for damages resulting from the use of the information contained herein.

First Edition

ISBN: 978-1-937449-62-9 softcover

Published by

YAV PUBLICATIONS
Asheville, North Carolina

Books may be purchased in bulk for educational, business, fundraising, or sales promotional use. For information, please contact books@yav.com

Cover art and interior images by June Ellen Bradley

35798642

Published 2023
Printed and Assembled in the United States of America

Dedication

I express gratitude to Jackie Woods, who teaches us to grow and live our heart qualities in daily life.

I thank Adawehi Healing Center for the opportunity to offer classes for children over the past twenty years.

Acknowledgments

My appreciation goes to the Arts Council of Henderson County, NC, for the Artist in Schools grant for supporting my sharing the Stories, Music, and Imagery Process at Hendersonville Elementary School and FernLeaf Charter School.

My appreciation goes to the Tryon Fine Arts Center, NC, for the Be Inspired Grant that supported my sharing the Stories, Music, and Imagery Process at Sunny View Elementary School.

My appreciation goes to the Arts Council of Henderson County, NC, for the Regional Artist Project Grant to support the preparation of the manuscripts for publication.

Thank you, Chris Yavelow, for your expertise and patience.

Thank you, Jennifer Mathews, for your clarity, willingness, and support.

I thank all the children who experienced the stories and gave feedback. I thank the parents who brought children to classes.

Access the Music Files

From the E-Book

Click the on-screen link following the specific example.

From the Print Book

Stream from the online player at LindaPowellsmi.com.

Or use the following QR Code to load the same player.

Alternatively, purchase the CD of all examples from:

StoriesMusicAndImagery.com

Contents

Acknowledgments vii
Preface xiii
Introduction 1
Character Education Programs 1
Character Traits 1
This Book Includes 3
The Stories, Music, and Imagery Process 5
Six Components of the Stories, Music, and Imagery Process 7
    Setting 7
    Stories 7
    Relaxation 8
    Directions 9
    Music 9
    Sharing 9
Overview of 20 Stories 11
    Younger Children 11
    Older Children 12
Benefits of the Stories, Music, and Imagery Process 13
    Creativity 13
    Goals 13
    Positive Social Interactions 14
    Self-Esteem 15
Role of the Adult 17
    Be a Role Model 17
    Honor the Child 18
    Listen Actively 19

Balancing the Inner and Outer Journey................................ 21
Frequently Asked Questions... 23
Overview and Checklist... 25
    The Setting: Prepare the Room 25
    Prepare the Children 26
    Read the Story... 26
    Guide the Relaxation 26
    Give the Directions 27
    Play the Music... 27
    Encourage the Sharing.. 27
Conclusion 29

Stories for Younger Children... 31

    Beauty 33
    Clearing 41
    Cooperation 47
    Confidence 55
    Friendship 61
    Growth.. 67
    Honesty 73
    Patience 79
    Support 87
    Trust 91

Stories for Older Children 97

    Acknowledgment. 99
    Appreciation 109
    Choice 117
    Communication. 123
    Expression. 131
    Focus 141
    Gratitude. 151
    Persistence. 157
    Possibilities 165
    Respect. 171

About the Author 177
About the Illustrator 179

Preface

The *Stories, Music, and Imagery Process* encourages children to explore their imagination, creativity, and self-awareness. I created this process combining original stories, relaxation, focused attention, reflection during classical music, and sharing time with drawing, writing, or verbally communicating their experience.

My first book, *Stories, Music, and Imagery: A Doorway to a Child's Self-Esteem,* was written for the children I taught in the Atlanta Public Schools. My intent was to motivate children to discover their own self-worth and grow their self-esteem. This book included 20 original stories, classical music corresponding to each story, and directions for guiding relaxation and sharing. This book is being used by parents, teachers, counselors, and therapists in the United States and abroad.

The response was so positive that I decided to create a second book, *Character Education through Stories, Music, and Imagery*, that applies this process to character education traits. This book includes 20 new stories, corresponding classical music, and directions to encourage children to recognize and grow their own character traits.

The *Stories, Music, and Imagery Process* brings together the power of the story, benefits of relaxation, clarity of focused attention, beauty of music, wisdom of the child, and support of the adult.

Access the Music Files

From the E-Book

Click the on-screen link following the specific example.

From the Print Book

Stream from the online player at LindaPowellsmi.com.

Or use the following QR Code to load the same player.

Alternatively, purchase the CD of all examples from:
StoriesMusicAndImagery.com

Introduction

CHARACTER EDUCATION PROGRAMS

Character traits are the integral inner qualities that help make each child unique. Different names have been used to describe these inherent traits. Heart qualities, values, virtues, principles, and attributes of the soul are but some of them. The *Stories, Music, and Imagery Process* provides children with a safe space, and supports them in recognizing and unfolding these qualities.

Schools recognize the importance of including character education programs as part of their curriculum. These programs add depth to the learning process and support each child's participation in the learning experience. *Character Education through Stories, Music, and Imagery* can be used to enhance existing character education programs in schools. Parents, counselors, therapists, camp leaders, or anyone who works with children may use this book with groups or individuals.

CHARACTER TRAITS

As young children are growing physically, they are also growing in their awareness of the world around them. Character education works on an inner level, helping to guide this expansion of awareness as each child discovers his/her own blend of unique qualities.

Character qualities can guide choices. A child who is aware of their inner qualities has the ability to follow inner guidance, and use discernment when making decisions. These decisions could range from clothing, to friends, to life goals, and to challenges. Character traits are like a compass, reminding a child who they are deep inside. These traits form the foundation for how they express themselves in daily life, enabling them to connect to their true nature, and be centered in who they are.

Many distractions in our society tug at a child's focus: peer pressure to look or act a certain way, to play a certain game, to own a certain piece of technology, and so much more. A child may be tempted to try to be like someone else and mimic how they act. These imitations of others may run contrary to the very nature of the child and offer little satisfaction. A child who is aware of their character qualities has a different perspective. These qualities are like a yardstick for measuring what fits, and what nurtures their true self. When there is a space and place for a child's inner awareness, the child can unfold to their true potential, and bring their special gifts into daily life.

Children grow and mature physically. With awareness, their character qualities may also grow. An adult guide in character education is like a gardener who nurtures a seed and cares for a plant as it matures and blooms. The *Stories, Music, and Imagery Process* gives children the space and place to get to know their unique character traits and encourages them to get to know themselves on a deeper level.

This book includes

- ✔ Introductory material.
- ✔ Description of the *Stories, Music, and Imagery Process*.
- ✔ Twenty original stories.
  - ☞ Ten stories for younger children (suggestion: K through 3rd grade).
  - ☞ Ten stories for older children (suggestion: 4th grade and older).

Each story includes

- ✔ A relaxation at the end of each story to encourage each child to quiet their body, emotions, and mind.
- ✔ Directions for each child to interact with the story and discover its personal meaning.
- ✔ A selection of classical music to be played at the end of each story's directions.
- ✔ A guide to encourage each child to share their experience through drawing, writing, or verbalizing.

THE STORIES, MUSIC, AND IMAGERY PROCESS

THE PROCESS

The *Stories, Music, and Imagery Process* brings together the power of the story, the benefits of relaxation, the clarity of focus, the beauty of music, the wisdom of the child, and the support of the adult.

The adult reads the story, relaxation exercise, and directions. The children discover what the story means to them by listening to a piece of classical music correlated to the story and then drawing, writing, or verbally sharing about their experience.

The *Stories, Music, and Imagery Process* encourages children to relate personally to the characters in the stories, and to use their imagination as a tool to get to know themselves better. Drawing, writing, and/or verbally sharing at the end of the process encourages expression and application of their discoveries.

The word "imagery" includes more than just visual pictures. Imagery also refers to memories, emotions, sensations, feelings, sounds, understandings, and awareness. Sometimes these come in symbols that can have meanings on several levels, giving depth to awareness. When children are relaxed, and their eyes are closed or in a soft stare, they can be in touch with the language of inner awareness.

Six Components of the Stories, Music, and Imagery Process

- ✔ Setting
- ✔ Stories
- ✔ Relaxation
- ✔ Directions
- ✔ Music
- ✔ Sharing

SETTING

The adult needs to prepare the space for the children with the intent of providing a safe place for exploring what is meaningful for them. The space needs to be quiet and protected from interruptions. The setting can be arranged so that children are seated or lying down, such as a classroom full of desks, an open space with carpet or mats, or a room with chairs.

STORIES

Ten stories for younger children explore the character traits of beauty, clearing, cooperation, confidence, friendship, growth, honesty, patience, support, and trust.

Ten stories for older children explore the traits of acknowledgment, appreciation, choice, communication, expression, focus, gratitude, persistence, possibilities, and respect.

Metaphors are used in these stories as vehicles for helping children connect something known to something new. Metaphors juxtapose a concept that children understand with a new perspective, allowing them to find relationships between what appear to be different ideas. During the reflective time following each story, the child can interact with the awareness, discover what the story means to them, and explore something new about themselves. The child can then apply these awarenesses to daily life.

RELAXATION

There are ten relaxation exercises included in this book. The adult guides the relaxation after each story. Relaxation helps children quiet the body, emotions, and mind; reduce stress, anxiety, tension; and prepare for focused attention. Relaxation helps children access imagery and experience, as well as their inner world of feelings, understandings, and awareness.

In order to activate the relaxation response in the child, the adult uses a slower voice tempo and rate of breathing, as well as a relaxed voice quality while reading the relaxation and directions. In this way, the process invites entrainment, a response where external rhythms affect internal rhythms. For example, the child's pulse and heart rates slow down to synchronize with the adult's relaxation and directions, and the music being played. When a child is relaxed, their feelings and imagery are more accessible.

DIRECTIONS

When the children are relaxed, the adult reads the directions to help the children discover what the story means to them. Children who are relaxed are ready to explore personal awareness.

MUSIC

Instrumental classical music was selected because it is complex enough to activate both hemispheres of the brain through specific melodic forms and patterns, recurring melodies, contrast, and change. Melody, harmony, rhythm, form, chord progressions, dynamics, style, instruments, pitch, and even the quality of performance can evoke different responses from the children. The music selections match the emotional tone of each story and support the feelings of the children.

These short pieces of music have a beginning, middle, and end that define the time for reflection. In addition to providing structure, they evoke imagery the children can use to explore the meaning of the story.

SHARING

When the music ends, the adult guides the children to bring their attention back to the room. The adult invites the children to express themselves in three practical ways. 1) Writing encourages children to find words to describe their experience. 2) Drawing offers them a chance to express through the medium of art; using color, shape, design, or pictorial representation. 3) Verbal sharing allows interaction between the adult and child. Sharing in these ways helps the children anchor their subjective experience into the objective world.

Children need to feel safe during sharing. They need to be heard without judgment or criticism that inhibit honest expression. Sharing time is a place where the listener honors the children by allowing them to express in their own way. Sharing is about the children's experiences, and the children's interpretation, not those of the adult listener.

The *Stories, Music, and Imagery Process* gives children the opportunity to go within and find a personal solution to daily challenges. Children who have this skill are more likely to use personally discovered solutions, rather than prescribed solutions imposed from outside themselves. Children have the ability to resolve many challenges in daily life. When allowed and encouraged, children can use their personal resources for problem solving, exploring new ideas, and finding ways to make positive changes in their lives.

In forty years of using this process, I am constantly amazed by the delight and wisdom of our children. Their smiles reflect that they enjoy the discovery of self-awareness. Their sharing shows the validity of their experience. Their comments reveal they like using their imagination in new ways:

"That's neat!"

"That was fun!"

"Let's do that again!"

Overview of 20 Stories

YOUNGER CHILDREN

Beauty	A girl discovers that beauty starts on the inside.
Clearing	A girl learns to let go of the old to make space for the new.
Cooperation	A boy learns to bring his talents and cooperate in a group.
Confidence	A girl learns teamwork instead of whining about her fear of losing a game.
Friendship	A boy learns about real friends.
Growth	A boy learns to trust his ability to grow and meet new challenges.
Honesty	A boy learns to tell the truth instead of blaming someone else.
Patience	A boy learns the value of waiting, instead of throwing a tantrum for what he wants in the moment.
Support	A boy realizes the many ways he receives a helping hand.
Trust	A girl learns to trust her ability to make friends in a new place.

OLDER CHILDREN

Acknowledgment	A girl learns to recognize her own beauty instead of trying to copy someone else's glamour from a magazine.
Appreciation	A girl learns to appreciate herself instead of criticizing and judging what she does not like.
Choice	A boy decides how he expresses himself.
Communication	A girl learns how to listen to what others are saying, instead of manipulating others in conversation.
Expression	A boy learns that he can accept himself and not worry about being more than or less than others.
Focus	A boy learns how to focus his attention instead of fantasizing.
Gratitude	A boy learns to see mistakes as an opportunity to grow.
Persistence	A girl learns to complete her homework and not give up because it is hard.
Possibilities	A girl discovers several ways to do her science project.
Respect	A boy learns to respect himself and others.

Benefits of the Stories, Music, and Imagery Process for Children

- ✔ Creativity
- ✔ Goals
- ✔ Positive Social Interactions
- ✔ Self-Esteem

CREATIVITY

The stories in this compilation that encourage creativity include: Clearing, Expression, Growth, and Possibilities.

The *Stories, Music, and Imagery Process* encourages children to use both sides of their brains. The left side of the brain focuses on intellect, logic, words, thoughts, and people, places, and things. The right side of the brain includes intuitive feelings, images, symbols, imagination, insight, and awareness. When right and left brain activities are combined, the potential for self-awareness and creative expression can be exponentially more effective.

GOALS

Stories that encourage children to see a larger purpose and strive for achievement are Focus, Growth, Patience, and Persistence.

These stories encourage children to learn to make healthy choices, see a bigger picture, and set long-range goals. Waiting for something in the future is different from instant gratification and requires a distinct perspective. It requires seeing a reason and purpose for long-term goals.

POSITIVE SOCIAL INTERACTIONS

Stories that encourage children to develop social skills are Choice, Communication, Cooperation, Friendship, Gratitude, and Support.

The characters in the stories are dealing with some of the same issues that children face in their daily interactions with family and friends. Children can learn from the experiences of the children in the stories. During the reflective time, while listening to the music, they can explore their own options and choices.

Dealing with and expressing emotions are key strategies when interacting with self and others. Children need guidance in learning how to deal with emotions in effective ways. Emotions themselves are not harmful. However, suppressed emotions can be harmful. Feelings that are stuffed, pushed aside, not expressed, or denied do not disappear. They continue to slosh around inside and are often acted out in harmful ways. Social interactions and educational opportunities may be blocked until the child is able to deal more effectively with these emotions.

Children need a safe place where they can learn to access and express their emotions in acceptable ways. The *Stories, Music, and Imagery Process* is a safe way for children to access and feel emotions. This is a space where they can experience their feelings honestly in the moment. Children who express and share emotions can own them, instead of acting them out. They have learned a technique that will serve them well throughout their lives.

SELF-ESTEEM

Stories that encourage children to recognize their intrinsic self-worth are Acknowledgment, Beauty, Confidence, Honesty, Respect, and Trust.

Each child is intrinsically worthy. Self-worth is validation from the inside. Self-esteem comes from children's discovery of their own inherent self-worth. It is important to remember that self-esteem is healthy love and appreciation of self, not narcissism or an unhealthy preoccupation with self. In these stories children focus on inner experience to discover validity and self-worth. When children explore and experience these qualities within, they can discover who they are and what they believe.

Children often look outside themselves for validity or to mimic a style or behavior in order to be popular. When looking outside of self for validity, self-worth can be compromised. Children who learn to accept and love themselves can be more accepting, kind, and nonjudgmental of others.

Role of the Adult in the Stories, Music, and Imagery Process

The role of the adult is to

- ✔ Be a Role Model.
- ✔ Honor the Child.
- ✔ Listen Actively.

BE A ROLE MODEL

Adults are the doorway through which children can view various ways of relating, thinking, believing, expressing, and acting in the world. Adults are models for children, no matter whether they are conscious of this or not. Actions speak louder than words because actions are observed before words are interpreted.

Each adult teaches not only a lesson plan or classroom objective, but also demonstrates attitude, perspective, and personal values. The way an adult functions in the world—along with his or her beliefs, attitudes, concepts, and personal truths—are what the child can observe and learn. When an adult comes from a clear, loving place, the child will sense this intention.

An adult can give a child a gift from the heart that will last throughout the child's life. Genuine gifts do not necessarily come wrapped in a gift box with ribbons and bows; they come wrapped in love, sent from the adult's heart to the heart of the child.

What are these gifts? They are attitudes, concepts, and beliefs about self. When an adult acts with an attitude of love and respect, the adult provides the child with an example of love and respect for self. Honoring a child with a respectful voice, thoughts, and actions provides the child with a model for how to behave respectfully towards self and others. When an adult listens to a child in a nonjudgmental way, the child has a model for listening to self in a noncritical way. When an adult communicates with honesty and integrity, the child has the opportunity to learn honesty and integrity.

HONOR THE CHILD

A metaphor of a seed can help us understand the essence of honoring. A gardener does not have to tell a seed how to grow, form a bud, bloom, or emit its fragrance and beauty. The role of the gardener is to provide the appropriate setting to nurture the seed and weed away what would harm the seedling.

A child is like a seed with a blueprint within. This inner wisdom will guide the growth of the child. Honoring the child means respecting their inner wisdom. Honoring the child also means listening and hearing what the child is experiencing, feeling, thinking, and saying. When an adult honors the child's experiences, emotions, thoughts, and words, then that adult is acknowledging the integrity of the child.

LISTEN ACTIVELY

Active listening requires focus, concentration, patience, and sensitivity. Since the focus of the listener is on the child, the listener needs to clear away any distracting thoughts, actions, personal feelings, judgments, or preconceptions that could get in the way of really hearing what the child is saying. Remember that listening does not mean interpreting.

When the intention of the listener is to be fully present with the child, then the listener can hear the child on many levels. The listener connects heart-to-heart, and can hear the words that are said, see visual clues, sense body language, and feel the child's emotions. Children might share any of the following: symbols, images, metaphors, emotions, awareness, insights, or ideas that they experienced while listening to the music. It might not be easy for a child to express and verbalize a non-verbal experience. The adult needs to give full attention to the child and listen with patience.

When a child shares written words, allow the child to express. When a drawing is shared, acknowledge the child's interpretation. When a child shares verbally, give the child space to talk.

A child might have a creative idea but not know how to act on this idea. An adult can help the child explore ways to bring the idea into a practical form in daily life. A child might find a symbol. The adult can encourage the child to explore its meaning. If a child has a new awareness, just listening to the child empowers that child.

When the child is expressing an emotion, an adult can listen from the heart, and experience through empathy what the child is feeling. A child's expression of emotion does not mean that the child is broken and needs fixing. The role of the adult is not to fix the child, but to listen. When the adult is fully present without judgment or criticism, the child receives the gift of support. By validating the child's emotions, adults can foster greater self-understanding and acceptance within the child. For example, when a child is allowed to be sad, the child can move through that sadness and not get stuck in the emotion. Giving a child a safe space where feelings are acknowledged is a gift. As adults, we cannot take away their experiences of life, but we can be there to give support and encouragement.

Balancing the Inner and Outer Journey

The *Stories, Music, and Imagery Process* gives children the opportunity to go on an inner journey to self-discovery. A child walks many paths in the outer world such as going to the store, a favorite place, or school. The inner journey is also a path. In the outer world, a child can follow a path to a store to shop for needed items. Likewise, a child can follow a path in the inner world to shop for an awareness of a talent, quality, or aspect of self. The inner world is full of resources and knowledge for the child to discover.

A child may have a favorite place in nature that is peaceful and quiet. A corresponding place exists in the inner world, where the child can access inner peace in times of stress. Just as a child follows a path to a teacher's room at school, so can a child follow a path in the inner world to a place of learning. For example, the child might see an image of a wise person, or a powerful animal that takes the form of inner guidance and wisdom.

The inner journey is one of self-discovery and self-awareness. A child who knows how to enter the inner world can access unique abilities. Perhaps a child is facing a test, classroom presentation, recital, or baseball game. A child who knows how to enter the inner world and connect with the quality of courage is able to access courage needed for challenging situations. Such a child uses inner strengths for success in daily life. This is an example of a healthy balance between the inner and outer worlds.

In contrast, a child who focuses on the inner world to the neglect of the outer world could be a daydreamer who looks out of the window and misses important classroom learning. A daydreamer does not connect to the outer world, and does not know how to bring inner awareness to outer life in a practical way. Conversely, a child who makes personal choices solely based on peer pressure, commercial advertising, or other outside influences is not in touch with the inner sense of self and personal values.

The *Stories, Music, and Imagery Process* helps children integrate the people, places, and things in their lives (the outer focus) and their feelings and personal experiences about them (the inner focus). This integration completes the circle, sparks creativity, and allows children to use the process to discover something new about themselves. By bringing together the external and the internal, events and feelings, and knowledge and intuition, children can balance these aspects, and find a sense of stability.

A balance between the two worlds is necessary for a child to develop into a well-functioning and responsible adult. A child with the ability to enter both the inner and outer worlds can draw upon inner awareness and relate to daily life in effective, practical, and successful ways.

Frequently Asked Questions

What if the child can't get in touch with the inner experience?

Time and experience may be needed for some children to discover their imagination. Some children spend many hours staring at TV, movies, computer games, and commercial advertising. These are passive experiences which are different from the creative experience of discovering the power of one's own imagery. Listening to a story, imagining the looks of the characters, and then experiencing one's own imagery engages the creative facilities of the child. An artist imagines a picture that will be painted on blank canvas. An architect has an inner vision of what a finished building will look like before drawing blueprints. A child can also develop skills of imagination so that what is conceived in inner images and experiences can then be brought into outer form on the screen of life. This is a learned life skill that prepares the child for success. The *Stories, Music, and Imagery Process* gives children the time and experience needed to develop this skill.

What if my child is a daydreamer?

The *Stories, Music, and Imagery Process* gives the child tools to explore the inner experience safely and apply inner awareness to daily life. These abilities will assist the child in harnessing creative ideas for practical application in daily life. Learning to access both inner and outer experience empowers the child.

Is the Stories, Music, and Imagery Process therapy?

The *Stories, Music, and Imagery Process* is not therapy, nor is it intended to be therapy. If serious issues arise, then contacting a parent or teacher support team in the school is recommended. The purpose of the *Stories, Music, and Imagery Process* is to develop self-awareness, confidence, and self-esteem, as well as to discover ways to apply insights in daily life.

Overview and Checklist

OVERVIEW OF THE STORIES, MUSIC, AND IMAGERY PROCESS

- ✔ Adult prepares the setting.
- ✔ Adult reads the story.
- ✔ Adult gives the relaxation.
- ✔ Adult reads the directions.
- ✔ Adult plays the piece of classical music.
- ✔ Adult invites the child to share the experience.

THE SETTING: PREPARE THE ROOM

- ✔ Choose a space that is free from distractions and noise.
- ✔ Choose soft lighting.
- ✔ Create a comfortable space.
- ✔ Use chairs, carpet, mats, beanbags, pillows, or stuffed animals, or allow children to put their heads on their desks.
- ✔ Use a good sound system to play the music.
- ✔ The adult sets definitions and boundaries, so that the children know what to expect. Here are some suggestions.
  - ☞ This is your quiet space.
  - ☞ Respect the space of others.
  - ☞ Be careful not to disturb others in any way.
  - ☞ We respect self and others.
  - ☞ This is a quiet time for listening.
  - ☞ Focus on your experience and use your imagination.

PREPARE THE CHILDREN

To prepare the child, the facilitator may want to share the following with the children.

- ✔ You will hear a story about a child your age.
- ✔ You will have a chance to relax and become quiet.
- ✔ During some beautiful music, you can reflect on what the story means to you. This is a time to discover something new about you.
- ✔ At the end of the music you can write or draw or tell about your experience.

READ THE STORY

- ✔ Use a soft voice.
- ✔ Pronounce words clearly.
- ✔ Speak in a slow, relaxed tempo.

GUIDE THE RELAXATION

The adult can facilitate relaxation.

- ✔ Use a soft, gentle voice.
- ✔ Allow words to flow smoothly.
- ✔ Use a slower tempo of speaking.
- ✔ Use a calm, relaxed voice.
- ✔ Feel relaxed and free from tension.
- ✔ Ask each child to find a comfortable position.
- ✔ Ask each child to allow his/her body to be quiet.
- ✔ Ask each child to allow his/her breathing to be very quiet.
- ✔ Read the relaxation script for the story.
- ✔ Pause at appropriate times.

GIVE THE DIRECTIONS
- ✔ Read the directions in a clear voice.
- ✔ Pause at appropriate times.
- ✔ Have confidence that the directions will encourage the child to interact with the essence of the story.

PLAY THE MUSIC
- ✔ Be sure the music is the one designated for that story.
- ✔ Be sure the volume is at a comfortable level.
- ✔ Begin the music.
- ✔ Accept no distractions during the music.
- ✔ Know that the music is three to four minutes in length.

ENCOURAGE THE SHARING
- ✔ When the music is over, softly say, "The music has ended. Gently bring your attention back to the classroom."
- ✔ Since some children may be relaxed and feel sleepy, give the children time to bring their attention back to the classroom.
- ✔ Offer a choice of writing, drawing, or verbal sharing. Writing and drawing require more time than verbal sharing.
- ✔ Have paper, pencils, markers, and/or crayons available if you choose writing or drawing.
- ✔ Allow time for the children to share with the teacher, with each other, and/or with the group.
- ✔ Honor each child by giving full attention to his or her expression.
- ✔ Do not interpret the child's experience. This is the job of the child.

- ✔ Be patient.
- ✔ Support and encourage the child to discover his or her own meaning.
- ✔ Keep your focus on the child.
- ✔ Ask appropriate questions such as:
    - ☞ "What was that like for you?"
    - ☞ "How did you feel?"
    - ☞ "Does that remind you of something in your life?"
    - ☞ "What does that mean to you?"
    - ☞ "What would you like to do with what you have discovered?"

Conclusion

The *Stories, Music, and Imagery Process* involves creative expression based on personal experience. The process encourages the child to become deeply acquainted with self in a setting of safety and respect where each child is honored. A child with the ability to travel both inner and outer awareness paths can find balance and confidence. The child can then experience and discover self-worth.

This process helps the child become more aware of the qualities of the inner self, and to experience self-worth and self-trust. In a world where acceptance is manipulated by the media and peer pressure, it is essential for a child to have a sense of self that will not be pulled off center by what others say. When character education qualities are developed from within, the child is guided by their inner compass to lead a more balanced and self-actuated life.

Access the Music Files

From the E-Book

Click the on-screen link following the specific example.

From the Print Book

Stream from the online player at LindaPowellsmi.com.

Or use the following QR Code to load the same player.

Alternatively, purchase the CD of all examples from:

StoriesMusicAndImagery.com

Stories for Younger Children

Beauty

Gail sat alone in her room and looked out the window at her older brothers and sisters playing in the yard. Her two sisters wore beautiful scarves and had tiaras in their hair, just like real princesses. Her two older brothers were knights.

A tear rolled down Gail's face. She quickly wiped it off when her mother walked into her room. "Why aren't you playing with your brother and sisters?"

"They won't let me play with them. They say I'm not beautiful like a princess, and I'm skinny and my hair is like spaghetti."

"Oh, your brother and sisters are leaving you out because you're the youngest one. They haven't learned to see your beauty. Do you think what they say is true?" her mom asked.

"No . . . . well I hope it isn't. What if it's true and I don't grow up to be beautiful?"

"You can see your beauty now. You don't have to wait until you're older," her mom said. "I have a present for you," her mom said.

Gail watched her mom open a long, thin package and pull out a long handle with a round mirror on top. "Look at the beautiful little buds around the mirror," her mom said.

Gail put her finger on one of the little buds.

"You are like one of those beautiful buds. Each day you grow bigger," continued her mom. "You will have many more birthdays as you grow taller and open like a bud into a flower."

Gail smiled.

"You are beautiful each day of your life. You don't have to wait until you're grown up to be beautiful. This mirror reflects your beauty. When you look into your eyes, look even deeper to see how your beauty shines through your eyes. When you look at your face, see how your inner beauty radiates through your skin," she said.

Gail smiled at her reflection in the mirror and said, "Thanks, Mom!"

"Would you like to hear a story?" her mom asked.

"Yes," Gail said, as she held her mirror carefully in her hands.

"This is a story about a princess and her mirror that she called her looking glass."

Once up on a time there was a princess who lived in a beautiful castle surrounded by a moat. The princess was sad for she had lost something precious. Her mother, the queen, had given her a present for her birthday.

"Here is a magic looking glass," the queen said, as she gave the gift to the princess. "It is magic because when you gaze into the looking glass, you can see your inner beauty."

The princess treasured her looking glass and handled it carefully so that no harm could come to it. Every day she looked at her inner beauty. There came a time when she began to think that only the looking glass could show her beauty. She even thought her beauty was in the looking glass.

One day she dropped her looking glass, and the broken pieces fell all over the stone floor. She tried to pick up each sliver of glass and put them together again. It didn't work.

The princess cried and sobbed, "I lost my beauty."

That night her Fairy Godmother heard her crying and came, but the princess was crying so hard that she was not even aware that her Fairy Godmother was in her room.

Finally, the princess cried herself to sleep and was quiet. The Fairy Godmother looked at the princess and thought, How can I tell her that the looking glass did not hold her beauty; it only reflected her inner beauty. She has beauty on the outside because she is first beautiful on the inside.

The Fairy Godmother took out her magic wand, tapped it three times, and waved it over the sleeping princess. At that moment, the princess began to dream that she was alone in a deep forest.

"I'm lost," the princess said. "I'm afraid. How can I find my way home?"

She turned in a circle and saw a path on the other side of a big tree. "Maybe this path will take me home."

She followed the path to the edge of the forest where a large meadow spread out before her. The sun was shining in the sky, a soft breeze blew through her hair, and birds were singing.

"This is a beautiful place," she whispered, and started to sing, "Sun, you are so beautiful; wind, you are so beautiful; birds, you are so beautiful."

'Princess, you are so beautiful,' were the words that she heard. She stopped and looked around. She saw the sun, felt the breeze and heard the birds. She did not see anyone else. She began to dance and sing again, "Sun, you are so beautiful; wind, you are so beautiful; birds, you are so beautiful." Again, she heard the words, 'Princess, you are so beautiful.'

The princess stopped to look around a second time. "Where did that voice come from?" She turned around and didn't see anyone.

The princess sat down, became very quiet, and listened. She heard the words, 'Princess, you are so beautiful.' She opened her eyes. She looked around and still didn't see anyone.

"Maybe I'm imagining that someone is telling me I'm beautiful." She closed her eyes again and heard the words, 'Princess, you are beautiful.'

"Who are you?" the princess asked.

"I am your inner princess," the voice answered.

"What's an inner princess?"

"Before there can be an outer princess, there has to be an inner princess. Think about the songs of the birds. Their song starts inside and then they sing it to the world. Your beauty starts on the inside and shines out to the world. Your beauty is deep inside of you, fills your body, and then your beauty can be seen by the world."

The princess stood up and smiled. She opened her eyes and began to dance and sing, "I have an inner princess. My beauty is deep inside of me."

The next morning the princess woke up and said, "I feel different this morning." She stretched and stood up.

She saw the broken looking glass pieces on her table and said, "It's time to throw this broken glass away. My beauty is not in my looking glass. I have a beautiful princess inside of me." The princess began to dance around her room. She danced a beautiful dance because she was dancing her beauty deep inside of her.

Gail smiled at her mom. "I like that story about the beautiful princess."

Her mom hugged her and said, "Remember, you have an inner princess who is beautiful. Your mirror reflects your beauty and reminds you that your beauty is deep inside of you."

Beauty: Relaxation and Directions

RELAXATION: SMILE

Allow yourself to smile.

> *(pause)*

Notice how your smile feels in your body.

> *(pause)*

Feel the feeling behind your smile.

> *(pause)*

DIRECTIONS

Imagine a mirror in front of you.

> Notice its size.
>
> > (pause)
>
> Notice its shape.
>
> > (pause)
>
> Notice its color.
>
> > (pause)

As the music begins, look into the mirror and notice something beautiful about yourself.

MUSIC

Play *Clair de Lune from Suite Bergamasque* by Debussy.
4:24 minutes

At the end of the piece of music, softly say, "The music has ended. Gently bring your awareness back to this room."

SHARING

1. Write about your experience.

    or

2. Draw your experience.

    or

3. Tell about your experience.

Clearing

Clearing

Lily's mom stood in the doorway to Lily's room, folded her arms, and shook her head. Lily was standing in her room because there was no place to sit. As she looked around the room, Lily's mom sighed and said, "What a mess. What are you going to do, Lily?"

Lily looked at the piles of clothes on the floor. Her books were piled so high on the bookshelf that some slid on to the floor. Pajamas were hanging out of a dresser drawer. The closet door would not close because shoes were in the way. Toys were all over her bed and the floor. Lily couldn't even see all the stuff under the bed. "How can I ever clean up this mess?" she asked.

"Sort it. Start with one item at a time," her mother said.

"Sort it?" Lily asked.

"Sorting means you take one item at a time and ask the question 'Does this match who I am now?' If it doesn't, you can put it in a box to give away. I'm going to get a big box for all the stuff you don't want or don't need," her mom said. "I'll take this box to the thrift store for some younger girls who need what you give away."

Lily looked at her books first. There were too many to fit on her bookshelf. She picked up one book, *The Little Engine That Could*. "I like this book because it reminds me that I can do something hard if I think I can." She put the book on the shelf. Lily picked up another book and said, "This book is for babies."

Lily's mom came to her room with a box. "Here's a book some baby would like," Lily said as she put the book into the big box.

"I'm sure you'll find more things you have outgrown. When you're finished sorting the books, clear out the toys you no longer use. I will come back later to see your room."

Soon the bookcase was neatly filled with books. Lily smiled as she said, "These are the books I like the most and will want to read again."

Next Lily looked at the toys all over the floor. *I left some of them there because I really didn't want them anymore,* she thought. *These toys went into the big box first.* She sorted out some toys from her toy chest as she thought, *These were fun to play with when I was little and I don't play with them now.* She carried these toys into the big box and kept the ones she enjoyed.

She looked at her closet shelf full of games and thought, *This will be easy. Some of these games are for little girls, and I'm too old for baby games.* She put several games into the big box.

Lily looked at her neat bookshelf, toy box, closet, and smiled. Then she turned to her dresser drawers with her pajamas hanging out. She removed the old ones that were too small and folded the rest into neat stacks. She pulled open the bottom drawer and realized, *I have not worn these jeans because they only reach my ankles.* She put the jeans and old pajamas into the box.

Next, she looked at her tops. *I don't like this color, and these are too small. I'm not sure about this one. I'd better try it on.* Lily looked into the mirror and thought, *It just doesn't feel right.* She took off the top and put it in the to go pile. She continued to sort through her tops, then carried a huge pile of them to the big box.

She arranged the tops she wanted to keep in the drawer beside the pants that were long enough. Next, she sorted through her socks, underwear, and dresses. She kept only the best ones.

"Mom, come and look at my room," Lily called.

Her mom came to her room, looked around and said, "Wow, you did such a great job and you filled up this big box."

"Yes," Lily said. "I just kept what I really like, and what fits me now."

"You cleared the clutter. Now you have space to explore what you are like now that you are older."

"What do you mean?" Lily asked.

"When you get rid of the little girl things, you have space to grow into who you are becoming."

"Who am I becoming?" Lily asked.

"That's for you to discover. When I look at you, I see your beauty, joy, and love of life. What do you see?"

Lily looked into her mirror and said, "I'm taller now. I don't look like a little girl anymore."

She looked into her eyes and asked, "Who do I want to be?"

"You have a bigger space to explore that question," her mom said. "Spend some time with yourself. I'll take this big box out of your room."

Lily looked into the mirror again and wondered, *I cleared out my little girl things. I'm no longer a little girl. What do I want?*

Lily walked over to the top dresser drawer and took out her diary and pen. She sat down and began to write.

"Dear Diary. I'm no longer a little girl. I cleared out my little girl things and I'm ready to grow. Let me tell you some ideas I have about the bigger me. I know you will understand what I have to say."

Lily wrote her new thoughts and feelings into her diary.

Clearing: Relaxation and Directions

RELAXATION: TENSE AND RELEASE (SHORT)

Find a comfortable position for your body.
(pause)

Allow your body to become quiet.
(pause)

Lift one leg a few inches off the floor – hold.
(pause)

Then allow the leg to relax and gently return to the floor.
(pause)

Lift the other leg a few inches off the floor – hold.
(pause)

Then allow the leg to relax and gently return to the floor.
(pause)

Now make a fist with one hand and hold.
(pause)

Then allow the muscles of your hand and arm to relax.
(pause)

Now make a fist with the other hand and hold.
(pause)

Then allow the muscles of your hand and arm to relax.
(pause)

Raise your shoulders toward your ears.
(pause)

Then allow your shoulders relax.

> *(pause)*

Squint your eyes as if the sun were bright.

> *(pause)*

Then relax the muscles of your face.

DIRECTIONS

In your imagination, look around your room.

Look at your dresser, closet, floor, and under your bed.

Is there something you have outgrown?

Is there something that no longer fits who you are now?

When the music begins, clear out what you have outgrown to make space for the new you.

MUSIC

Play #13 *Hornpipe from Concerto Grosso, Op. 6 No.7,* by Handel
2:36 minutes

At the end of the piece of music, softly say, "The music has ended. Gently bring your awareness back to this room."

SHARING

1. Write about your experience.

> *or*

2. Draw your experience.

> *or*

3. Tell about your experience.

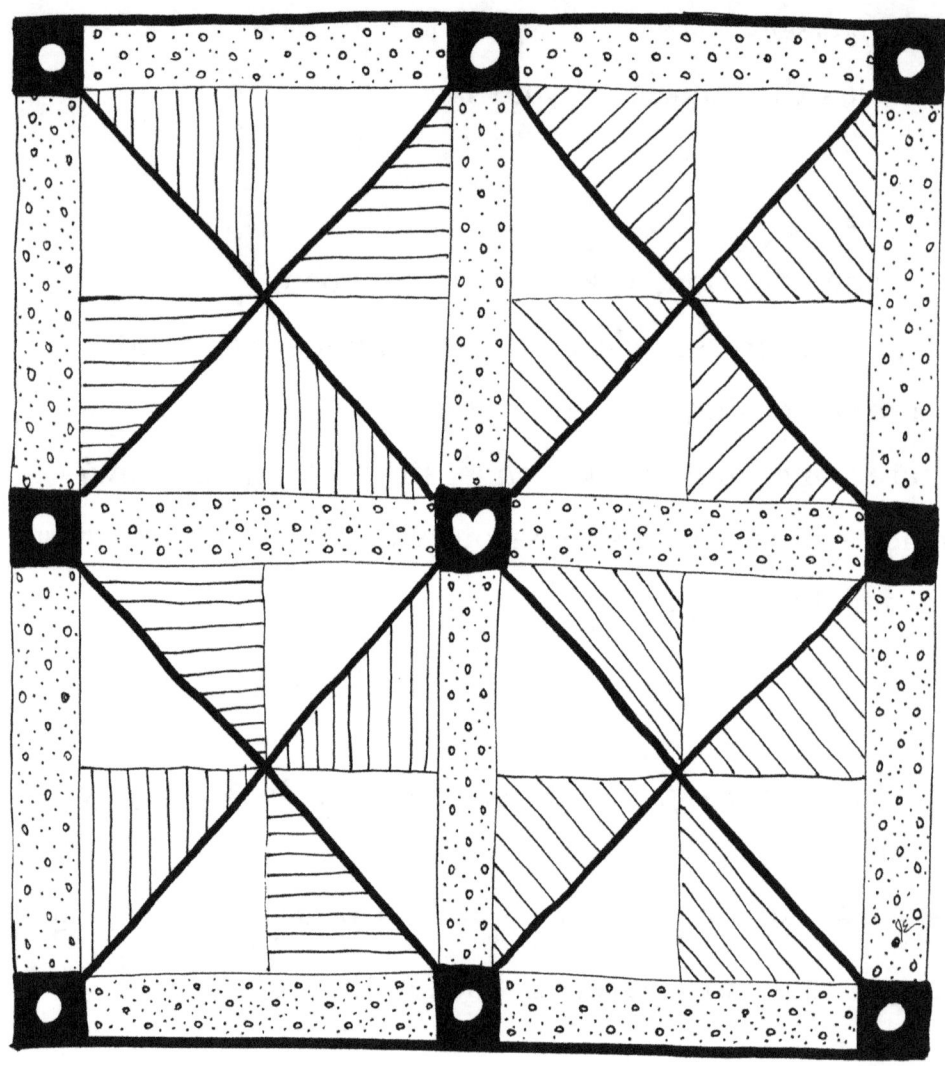

Cooperation

Cooperation

Damien sat all by himself under a tree near the playground. He frowned, and his shoulders drooped forward as he watched his friends play ball. Well, they had been his friends. He wasn't so sure they were his friends now. *Why won't they include me?* he wondered. *Why don't like me?*

The children cheered and jumped up and down. *That must be the team that won the game*, thought Damien. The players left the ball field, and some passed by as if they had not seen him. Damien heard them talking and realized, *Even the team that lost looks like they are having a good time.*

Jason walked toward Damien, stopped, and said, "I'm not mad at you."

"All the others are mad at me," Damien said.

"No, they're not. They're just frustrated because you argue with everyone," Jason said.

"What do you mean?" Damien asked as he folded his arms.

"You always want everything your way," Jason said.

Well, my way is best, thought Damien, but he didn't say this out loud.

Jason continued, "You have some good ideas, and so do I, and so do our friends. We just need to take turns. You can't expect us to do what you want to do all the time."

Damien held his lips tightly together. He did not answer. "Come walk with me to my house," Jason said. "I have something to show you." Damien nodded, stood up and walked beside Jason.

"What is it?" Damien asked.

"My grandma is visiting. Come to my room. I have something to show you," Jason said. Damien followed Jason inside. They walked up the stairs and down the hallway. Jason opened his door and said, "There it is."

Damien looked around and wondered, *What am I supposed to see*?

Jason went over to his bed and pointed to the quilt. "Here it is."

Damien walked over, looked at the quilt, and said, "That's a cool pattern. It was nice of your grandma to buy it for you," Damien said.

"She didn't buy it. She made it," Jason proudly said.

"How did she make it?" Damien asked.

"She and her friends made the quilt. They took pieces of cloth and stitched them together. Look closely." Damien bent over to get a closer look. He saw little triangles that were sewn together with teeny tiny stitches to made squares. "Each stitch is made with a needle and thread," Jason explained.

"There must be hundreds of stitches in this one little square," Damien said.

"There must be thousands of stitches in the bigger squares," Jason said, he looked at the large quilt that covered the whole bed. "Would you like to meet my grandma?" Jason asked.

"Sure," Damien said. Jason walked out of his room and Damien followed him down the hall.

He stopped at the next door and knocked. "Come on in," his grandma said. Jason opened the door, and the boys walked into the room. An older lady sat in a chair in front of a large square frame. She was pulling a needle and thread through some fabric.

"Hello boys. Is this a friend of yours?" she asked as she looked at her grandson.

"Yes, this is my friend, Damien," Jason answered.

"I'm glad to meet you," she said as she looked at Damien. Her eyes were gentle, and her voice was strong.

"May I see what you are doing?" Damien asked.

"Sure, come over and take a closer look," she answered. Damien walked over and looked. "See this needle with thread in it?" Damien nodded. "Here are the patches of material," she explained. "I take the cloth and fold it this way." Damien watched her nimble fingers shape the cloth into a triangle. "I place the cloth on the backing like this and stitch around the triangle to secure it to the backing that is held in place by this wooden frame."

"You have a long way to go. That triangle is so small, and the quilt will be so big," Damien said.

"Yes, it takes time and patience to make a quilt one piece at a time," Grandmother explained.

"I hear voices coming down the hall," Jason said.

"Yes, they're my friends who are coming to help make this quilt," Grandmother said.

Damien looked at the doorway and in came six women. Some were tall, some were short, some were older, and some were younger. Some wore dresses, and some wore jeans.

"Pull up your chairs," Grandmother said. There was a lot of shuffling as the women brought their chairs over to the frame. When they were seated, Grandmother said, "Meet Damien. He's a friend of my grandson, Jason." The women looked at Damien and smiled.

Grandmother continued, "He has never seen quilting before. Let's show him how we make a quilt together." The women got out their needles, threads and scissors. They each picked up a piece of fabric, folded it into a triangle, and began to stitch it to the backing.

"How do you know where to put the fabric?" Damien asked.

"We agreed on one pattern," one lady answered.

"How do you all agree?" Damien asked.

"We all have different ideas. Each person shares and then we choose one," Grandmother explained. "We picked the pinwheel pattern for this quilt."

"What colors do you use?" Damien asked.

"Each person brings some fabric and we select colors that fit together. The rest of the fabric can be used for another quilt. This quilt is for a friend whose bedroom is green and yellow. These colors will match her room."

"Oh," Damien said as he watched the women stitch their cloth triangles together. "This quilt will take a long time to make," Damien said.

"That's OK," said a lady in a red shirt. "We like to meet and work together. It's fun to sit beside my friends and make something beautiful together."

"Quilting is one of my favorite things to do," said the lady beside her. "It's exciting to work together." The lady next to her said, "I like to see the patterns."

"I like the way we talk," said a lady in a yellow shirt. "We can make decisions without arguing."

Damien looked at his watch and said, "I have to go now. Thanks for showing me how to make a quilt."

"Goodbye," the ladies said as Damien and Jason walked out the door.

Damien walked down the hallway and paused by Jason's room. He looked again at the quilt. "There are hundreds of pieces of fabric sewn together," observed Damien.

"Yes," Jason said as he looked at his quilt. "When I pull the quilt around me at night, I can feel the love that is stitched into my quilt."

"Wow," Damien said. "Your grandmother gave you a beautiful gift."

Jason nodded and smiled. Then he asked, "Are you coming to the playground tomorrow?"

"Yes, if the others will let me," Damien said.

"They will if you don't argue," Jason suggested.

"I won't argue with anyone tomorrow," Damien said. He walked down the steps, out the door, and up the street toward his home.

The next afternoon Damien walked toward the playground and thought, *I want to play baseball today, and I want to be the pitcher.*

Damien joined the other boys as they stood in a circle. "What do you want to play today?" Brian asked.

Keith spoke first and said, "Baseball."

"No, we played that yesterday," Brian said. "Let's play something different."

Damien was about to open his mouth to argue; then he shut his mouth as he remembered the quilt with its different colors.

David said, "Let's play dodge ball. I brought a ball we can use."

"OK," Keith said. "Who wants to be captain?"

John and Marty were the first to raise their hands.

"You two can be captains. Now pick a number from one to 10," Brian said.

Marty said, "Number three."

"Number six," John said.

"Ten is the number," Brian said. "John gets to pick first."

John looked around the circle, looked at Damien, and said, "I choose Damien."

When the two teams were chosen, Brian said, "John's team is in the center first."

As Damien went to the center with the rest of his team, he remembered Jason's grandma and her friends who worked together. *I'll work together with my friends today. I might even have more fun if I don't argue.*

Cooperation: Relaxation and Directions

RELAXATION: COUNTING BACKWARDS FROM 5 TO 1

We will count backwards from 5 to 1.

Begin with 5 as you notice how your body feels.

(pause)

Allow your body to become very quiet as I say 4.

(pause)

Find a way to be even quieter as I say 3.

(pause)

Your body is even more quiet as I say 2.

(pause)

Feel your body even more relaxed as I say 1.

(pause)

DIRECTIONS

When the music begins, remember a time when you joined a group and cooperated with a group decision. What piece did you bring to the group effort?

MUSIC

Play *Allegro from Concerto for 2 Horns in B flat major*, by Telemann.
2:52 minutes

At the end of the piece of music, softly say, "The music has ended. Gently bring your awareness back to this room."

Confidence

Confidence

"I can't do it. I'm so scared. When I mess up others will laugh at me," whined Janice in her most pitiful voice.

Her friends just looked at her. Nobody said anything. They just stared at her.

"You don't think I can do it either," Janice complained as tears welled up in her eyes.

"It's not that we don't think you can do it," her friend Tina said. "It's the way you say, 'I can't.' You use a whiny voice that's so annoying."

Joyce stood beside Janice and said, "I know how you feel, but as long as you use that 'poor me' voice, you won't be able to do anything at all. Do you remember what our soccer coach said?"

Janice frowned slightly as she said. "It was something about winning or losing."

"Yes," Joyce said, "It was back at the last practice when he told us that winning or losing is not as important as teamwork."

Tina added, "Remember when we played the team that won every game the whole season? We lost that game. Some of us felt like crying. Some of us did. Our coach said, "You played a great game. You had spirit, you worked together, you did your best. Teamwork is more important than winning a game."

"I remember what the coach said," Janice replied. "I just feel like I can't run fast enough or kick the ball as hard as others can."

"We are part of a team," Tina said. "You are not alone."

Joyce echoed, "You are not alone."

"We are part of a team," Tina said again. "Let's say it together. Joyce and Tina said, "We are part of a team." They looked at Janice, who joined them as all three said together, "We are part of a team."

"We are here to help each other," Joyce said. "Believe in yourself."

Janice smiled and said, "Thanks."

The three friends walked to the soccer field and Janice thought about what Joyce had said to her about her pitiful voice. *I guess I did whine. I wonder if my face looked as pitiful as I sounded. I don't even like to hear my own voice when I talk like that.*

Tina looked at Janice and said in a strong voice, "Remember when I kicked the ball to you and even though it was over to your right, you ran and kicked it toward the goal?"

Janice nodded her head.

Tina said, "Next time kick it to me, and I will be there to kick it into the goal."

"Let's practice this today," Joyce said.

The girls ran to the soccer field. The coach threw the ball toward Janice. She ran toward it and brought her foot back to kick the ball down the field. Joyce was there to kick the ball to Tina, who gave it a mighty kick to the goal.

"Good teamwork," the coach called.

That was fun, Janice thought. *I like running, and I know how to bring my foot back to kick the ball. I looked toward Joyce and the ball went right to her, and Tina was there to kick it toward the goal. Soccer is fun when I join my friends. I'm glad Joyce and Tina are my soccer buddies.* Janice felt taller and stood up straighter.

After the practice, the girls left the soccer field.

We played well, Janice thought. Then she said aloud, "We played well, and we had teamwork." The three girls walked arm in arm together.

Confidence: Relaxation and Directions

RELAXATION: BODY AWARENESS (SHORT)

Be aware of your feet.

(pause)

Be aware of your ankles.

(pause)

Be aware of your legs.

(pause)

Be aware of your hips and lower back.

(pause)

Notice how long your spine is from your lower back up to your neck.

(pause)

Be aware of your shoulders.

(pause)

Be aware of your arms.

(pause)

Be aware of your neck.

(pause)

Be aware of your mouth.

(pause)

Be aware of your nose.

(pause)

Be aware of your eyes.

(pause)

Be aware of your hair.

(pause)

DIRECTIONS

Remember a time when you felt confidence. Be aware of how your felt.

Be aware of your feeling of confidence.

MUSIC

Play #16 *Allegro from Horn Concerto No, 3 in E flat major*, K. 447, by Mozart.

3:38 minutes

At the end of the piece of music, softly say, "The music has ended. Gently bring your awareness back to this room."

SHARING

1. Write about your experience.

   or

2. Draw your experience.

   or

3. Tell about your experience.

Friendship

FRIENDSHIP

Daniel sat on the sofa and complained to his mom. "They don't like me," he muttered. "They always say things that hurt me. They're all against me."

"Who is against you?" his mom asked, as she sat in the chair next to him.

"Everybody," Daniel said, impatiently.

"Who is everybody?" his mom asked.

"Jesse and John always call me names," Daniel said in a low voice. "They make me feel bad."

"Nobody can make you feel a certain way," his mother said.

"But their words can," argued Daniel.

"Words can hurt only if you focus on their words and not who you really are," his mom explained.

"What do you mean?" Daniel asked.

"Give me an example. What did they say to you?" his mom asked.

"They said I'm stupid," Daniel said as his eyes got teary.

"Are you?" his mom asked.

"No, but they think I am," Daniel said in a louder voice.

"Who do you believe? Do you believe yourself, or Jesse and John?" his mom asked.

"Well . . . When they say it, I think it must be true," admitted Daniel.

"Do they know who you really are?" his mom asked.

"Well, no," Daniel said, shaking his head.

"Only you can know who you really are. You know you have a willingness to learn something new. You know how well you are doing in school. Why would you ever believe what they say?" his mom asked.

"I don't know. Suppose they are right?" Daniel inquired.

"Do you want them to like you?" his mom asked.

"Of course, they're my friends," Daniel said.

"When you try to please others, you focus on them instead of expressing who you are. Then you try to do what they want you to do," his mom explained.

"What do they want me to do?" Daniel asked.

"Believe their words so they will look better than you," his mom said.

"What do you mean?" Daniel asked

"Trying to feel better than another person is competition. In contrast, real friendship means appreciating and supporting each other," his mom explained.

"I want real friendship," Daniel said.

"Can you tell Jesse and John you want real friendship?" his mom suggested.

"How could I say it?" Daniel asked.

"Put it in your own words," his mom said.

"Maybe I could say I feel bad I feel when you call me stupid. I want a real friend," Daniel said.

"If they say yes, then you can have a real friend," his mom said.

"What if they say something else that hurts me?" Daniel asked.

"A bully is not your friend. Go and invite someone else to be your friend," his mom suggested.

"How long will it take? I don't want to be without friends forever," Daniel said.

"It won't be forever," encouraged his mom. "Trust yourself and your ability to make real friends."

"I need to talk to Jesse and John right now," Daniel said. He stood tall, opened the door, and walked outside to face Jesse and John.

"Hey Jesse! Hey John!" Daniel called. The boys stopped playing and came over to look at Daniel.

Daniel took a big breath and said, "When you call me stupid, I think you don't like me. I want friends who support me."

Jesse and John looked at each other.

Daniel continued, "If you are not willing to join me in friendship, I can find new friends."

Jesse and John burst out laughing.

"I thought we were just teasing," Jesse said.

"I guess we were being rude" John said.

"I want to be your friend," Jesse said as he held up his hand for a high five.

"Me too," John said. He held up his hand for a high five.

Daniel looked at Jesse, and he looked at John. He held up his hand. Together they joined in a high five of friendship.

Friendship: Relaxation and Directions

RELAXATION: LETTING GO OF TENSION

Allow your breath to become slow and steady.

(pause)

Notice a place in your body where there is tension or tightness.

(pause)

Breathe into that tense place.

(pause)

The next time you exhale, let go of some of that tightness.

(pause)

Each time you exhale, let go of more tightness.

(pause)

When that place in your body feels relaxed and comfortable, find another place in your body where there is tension and breathe into that tense place.

DIRECTIONS

When the music begins, choose one of your friends and realize how you appreciate and support each other.

MUSIC

Play *Adagio* from *Ballet Music: II from Faust* by Gounod.
3:50 minutes

At the end of the piece of music, softly say, "The music has ended. Gently bring your awareness back to this room."

SHARING

1. Write about your experience.

    or

2. Draw your experience.

    or

3. Tell about your experience.

growth

Growth

Jamie said goodbye to his teacher. This was a very special goodbye because it was the last day of school before the summer vacation. His teacher came over to him, looked directly into his eyes and said, "You have grown so much during this year. You are taller and have grown in your ability to read and write. May you continue to grow."

Jamie looked at his teacher and said, "Thank you for a great year. Goodbye."

He turned and walked out of the door of his classroom. Soon his smile turned into a frown as he realized, *This is the end of the last day of school. I won't be here all summer and I'll miss my teacher.*

That night when Jamie was getting ready for bed, he thought about the words of his teacher, "May you continue to grow."

After he brushed his teeth, he got into bed and put his head on his pillow. *What will I look like at the end of the summer? Will I be taller? Stronger?*

Jamie began to worry. *Will I be big enough for the next grade? Will I be smart enough? Will I be ready?* Finally, his eyes closed, and he fell asleep.

When Jamie woke up the next morning, he remembered a dream about a plant. He got dressed and went downstairs for breakfast. "Mom," he said as walked to the kitchen, "I had a dream last night. I dreamed about a plant that grew and had a flower."

"Tell me about your dream," his mom said as she put a plate of sliced apples on the table.

"First there was this seed in the dark ground. Then I saw roots go down and a stem go up. The stem grew taller and some leaves grew on the stem. Then a bud grew and opened up into a big flower."

"That sounds beautiful," his mom said.

"It was," Jamie answered.

"You are kind of like that plant," his mom said.

Jamie frowned and said, "What do you mean?"

"Think about it," his mom said as she turned to the stove to stir the oatmeal in the pan.

Jamie sat at the breakfast table and reached for the apple. He ate several slices, then his mom brought a bowl of oatmeal to the table.

Jamie ate a spoonful of oatmeal and said, "I know one way I'm like a plant. I grow bigger." Jamie said.

"Yes, you are taller. We had to buy bigger jeans because your old ones were too short."

Jamie smiled. "I like being taller. Soon I will be as tall as you."

"You have some growing to do before you are up to my chin," his mom said.

"I'll be that high before you know it."

His mom laughed, and then said, "Tell me about your roots."

"My roots?" Jamie asked.

"Yes, your roots. In your dream your plant had roots. Tell me about your roots."

"I don't have roots like a plant," Jamie said.

"In a way you do," his mom answered. "The roots bring water to the plant. You drink water. Your plant had roots in its home in the ground.

You have a home built on the ground. The plant takes in nourishment from the ground. You're eating a nourishing breakfast."

"Oh," Jamie said, thoughtfully.

"The plant is like a metaphor," his mom said.

"What's that?"

"It's a way to understand something by comparison," his mom said.

Jamie laughed as he said, "If I'm like a plant, have I bloomed?"

"What did you do in school?" his mom asked.

"I learned math and did well in my tests."

"That's blooming," his mom said.

"I did my science project," Jamie answered.

"That's like blooming."

"I passed my end of the year tests."

"That's blooming," his mom said.

Then Jamie was quiet for a few moments. He frowned, and then slowly asked his question, "Suppose I'm not ready for the next grade. Suppose I'm not big enough. Suppose I'm not smart enough."

His mom looked at Jamie and said, "The plant in your dream knows how to grow. You did not have to tell its roots to go down into the earth and its stem to go up. The plant knew how to grow bigger with new leaves and a flower. Jamie, there is a part of you that knows how to grow and bloom. Trust that part of you that knows how to grow."

Jamie nodded slowly. "I think I understand," he said. "I want to draw my plant with its big flower."

When he finished his breakfast, he went to his room. He got his paper and crayons and began to draw.

Growth: Relaxation and Directions

RELAXATION: STRETCHING

Stretch one leg.

(pause)

Now relax the muscles in that leg and notice how your leg feels.

(pause)

Stretch the other leg.

(pause)

Now relax the muscles in that leg and notice how your leg feels.

(pause)

Stretch one arm.

(pause)

Now relax the muscles in that arm and notice how your arm feels.

(pause)

Stretch your other arm.

(pause)

Now relax the muscles in that arm and notice how your arm feels.

(pause)

Stretch your spine from its base to where it joins your head.

(pause)

Now relax the muscles around your spine.

(pause)

Notice how long your spine is.

(pause)

DIRECTIONS

Imagine a seed with roots growing down and a stem that grows up. When the music begins, notice how your plant grows.

MUSIC

Play *Playful Pizzicato* from *Simple Symphony*, by Britten.
3:23 minutes

At the end of the piece of music, softly say, "The music has ended. Gently bring your awareness back to this room."

SHARING

1. Write about your experience.

   or

2. Draw your experience.

   or

3. Tell about your experience.

Honesty

HONESTY

"Look what I bought," Henry's mom said as she walked in the door.

Henry went over to his mom and saw she was holding a plant. "It has a pretty yellow flower on it," he said.

"Let's plant it outside," his mom said.

They walked outside to the yard and looked around. Henry pointed to the garage and said, "Let's plant it over there, so we can see it when we come up the driveway."

"That sounds good," his mom said. "The plant will be in the morning sun, so it will get the light it needs. Now we need a shovel."

"I'll get it," Henry called as he walked toward the garage. He came back with a shovel and started to dig. He pushed down with his foot, lifted up the dirt, and plopped it beside the hole. Henry continued to dig until the hole was several inches deep. "Is this deep enough?" he asked.

"Let's take the plant out of the pot and see." His mom tapped the sides and bottom of the pot, then carefully pulled out the plant. "Yes, it is. There's plenty of space for the roots." Henry and his mom carefully placed the plant into the hole and smoothed the ground around the plant.

"The plant needs water," his mom said.

"I'll get a watering can," Henry said. He went to the garage, filled the watering can with water, and carried it back to the plant.

"Pour the water gently all around the plant," his mom said, and Henry did so. "I think the plant will like it here," he said.

"I believe you're right," his mom said. "Let's go in inside for dinner. Remember Jimmy is coming over to play after dinner."

"Can we play ball in the yard?" Henry asked.

"Yes, you two play well together," his mom answered.

After dinner Henry and Jimmy went outside to play ball. Jimmy threw the ball first and Henry caught it and threw it back to Jimmy. They played until it started to get dark.

"Here's the last ball, can you catch this one?" Jimmy said as he threw the ball a little harder than he had planned.

Henry had to run to catch it. He ran back, and then took a few more steps backward. The ball bounced so he took another step back and caught the ball. Henry stopped and looked down. His eyebrows went up and his mouth opened to say "OH NO." The flower was broken off and was on the ground under his shoe.

Just then Henry's mother called to say, "Jimmy's mother is here, come inside now."

Henry took one more look at the broken plant and walked inside with Jimmy. After he said goodbye to Jimmy, he went right upstairs without looking at his mom.

"Are you going to bed already?" his mom asked.

"Yes, I'm tired."

"Go get ready for bed and I will come upstairs in a few minutes to say goodnight," his mom said.

Henry sat down on his bed and repeated, "What can I do? What can I do?"

He held his head with his hands and thought, *I could blame Jimmy. I could tell mom that Jimmy stepped on the plant and it was his fault the flower broke off. Mom could be mad at him and not me. But Jimmy is my friend. I don't want to lie about him. My mom might guess I'm lying. Or, I could just tell her it was an accident and that I'm sorry. Maybe she'll understand.*

Henry was in his pajamas when his mom walked into his room. "You have a frown on your face, is anything wrong?" his mom asked.

Henry took a deep breath and said, "Yes, I had an accident."

"What happened?" his mom asked as she sat beside him on the bed.

"Jimmy and I were playing ball and the last time he threw the ball I ran to catch it. It bounced, and I took another step back before I caught the ball. When I looked down, the new plant was broken."

"I'm so sorry that happened. It sounds like it was an accident. I know you liked the plant," his mom said. I'm not angry about the plant. I'm just glad you told the truth. You didn't blame it on Jimmy or make excuses. You were honest. Every time you tell the truth your honesty grows bigger and stronger. I'm very proud of you for being honest and telling the truth." She gave Henry a big hug.

"What will happen to the plant?" Henry asked.

"We'll look at it tomorrow when it is light. Maybe the roots will grow deep and send up another flower. If not, we can buy another plant. What is most important is that you have grown your honesty bigger."

Henry gave a sigh of relief and smiled. His mom smiled too. Henry felt much love coming from his mother's smile.

Honesty: Relaxation and Directions

RELAXATION: FOCUS ON YOUR BREATH

Be aware of your breath.

(pause)

Feel your breath going in and out, in and out.

(pause)

Notice how fast or slow your breath is going in and out, in and out.

(pause)

Gently feel your breath going in and out, in and out.

(pause)

DIRECTIONS

When the music begins, remember a time when you decided to be honest.

Notice how you felt. Notice what you did or said.

MUSIC

Play *Fast Movement* from *Guitar Concerto*, by Vivaldi.
3:23 minutes

At the end of the piece of music, softly say, "The music has ended. Gently bring your awareness back to this room."

SHARING

1. Write about your experience.

    or

2. Draw your experience.

    or

3. Tell about your experience.

Patience

Patience

"I want it now," wailed little Steven. Kendra and her mom looked at each other and sighed. They put their hands over their ears when Steven's wails turned into a piercing crescendo.

Kendra walked out of the room, and so did her mom. Steven followed them into the living room shouted, "Now, now, I want it now!"

His mom said, "Go to your room until you can talk to us without screaming."

"But I want my train now," wailed Steven.

"The answer is no," his mother said firmly. "You can't have it now. Go to your room and scream as much as you need to express your anger."

Steven stomped up the steps and hollered all the way to his bedroom.

"I can remember when you cried like that because you wanted a doll you saw in the store. I was so embarrassed that I picked you up and carried you out to the car," her mom said.

"I'm glad I grew up," Kendra said.

"You have done a lot of growing, and so has your patience," agreed her mom.

"What do you mean?" Kendra asked.

"You understand that some things take longer, and you have to wait patiently for them," her mom explained.

"Yes, but I don't like waiting," Kendra said.

"It's hard to wait," her mom said. "I'm waiting for the first daffodil to bloom after this long cold winter."

"I'm waiting for the blossoms on the dogwood trees," Kendra said.

"And the song of the robin when it returns in the spring," her mom said. "We can't hurry spring; it unfolds in its own time," her mom said.

"I can remember how I wanted my tooth to come out right away, so the tooth fairy could come," Kendra said.

Her mom smiled as she remembered Kendra as a little girl.

"I want to grow up and it is taking a long time to grow as tall as my big sister," Kendra said.

"Patience will help you grow through each year," reminded her mom.

Kendra frowned. Her mom continued. "You can grow patience each day."

"That's a hard job," Kendra said.

"When you rush in and say, 'I want it now,' you cut off your willingness to grow. Think of your piano. It has taken several years for you to be able to play your solo piece."

"Yes," Kendra said. "I had to learn the notes and rhythms, then my fingers had to learn to play the notes."

"You used patience to practice notes, rhythms, and fingering until you could play the music," her mom said.

They stopped to listen. "Steven is still crying," Kendra said.

"That's because his emotions want it now. He has to learn that a temper tantrum doesn't make it happen sooner."

Finally, the crying stopped, and Steven appeared at the top of the steps.

"Are you hungry?" his mom asked.

"Yes," sniffled Steven.

"Do you want to help make the pancakes?"

"Yes," Steven answered. He walked down the steps and followed his mom and Kendra into the kitchen.

"I'll measure the flour, and you can pour it into the mixing bowl," Kendra suggested.

Kendra carefully measured the flour and handed the cup to Steven. Kendra measured the rest of the dry ingredients, and Steven poured them on top of the flour.

"I'll hold the bowl and you can stir them together," Kendra said.

Steven picked up the large wooden spoon and stirred it slowly, so it wouldn't spill.

Their mother mixed the wet and dry ingredients in a big bowl and poured the batter onto the griddle. "Come watch the pancakes," she called.

Kendra pushed a chair over to the stove, so Steven could climb up and see.

"When will they be ready?" Steven asked.

"I know," Kendra said. "We watch for bubbles."

They watched and waited. And waited.

"You both are being very patient," their mom said.

Steven watched and waited. "Suddenly he shouted, "I see a bubble."

"I see it too," Kendra said.

When several more bubbles appeared, their mom took the spatula and peeked under one pancake. "They're brown on the bottom. Now it's time to flip them."

"Yum, they smell good," Steven said.

"It's time to set the table," their mom said.

Steven got off his chair and pushed it to the table. "I'll put the knife on the right side of the plate; you put the fork on the left side," Kendra said.

"The pancakes are ready," their mom said, as she put two on each plate.

Just then, Sandra walked through the door and said, "The pancakes smell so good."

"Come join us. Here's your plate," Kendra said to her big sister.

Steven smiled at his mom, then put a big piece of pancake into his mouth. "Your brother and sister are learning patience," his mom said.

"Patience is not easy to learn," Sandra said. I remember how it took me a long time to learn about the patience clock."

"What's a patience clock?" Kendra asked.

"There's clock time." Sandra pointed to the clock on the wall. "It's when something is scheduled to happen, like breakfast, or school. Then there is the patience clock – for the time it takes for long things to happen."

"Sandra, remember when you complained that you couldn't learn those new dance moves?"

"Yes, my teacher gave us a new dance, and I kept making mistakes and forgetting the next step. You told me to hold patience while my body learned it. I practiced the steps, and then one day my body remembered the moves and the dance flowed through me," Sandra explained.

"Yes, you gave your body time to integrate what was new, and bring all the pieces together. You brought patience to learning your dance," her mom explained.

"I have something to show you," Sandra said. She reached into her pocket. Steven and Kendra watched as she pulled something out and held it in her hand. She slowly opened up her hand to show them a smooth brown stone. "I carry a little stone in my pocket to remind me of patience," Sandra said.

"Look at this stone," Sandra continued. "It is thousands of years old. It reminds me of patience because its time clock is not the same as our clock time. Look at our clock on the wall. It ticks in seconds. The time clock of this stone must tick in centuries, so it can be thousands of years old."

Kendra and Steven looked at the stone as they tried to understand how long thousands of years must be. Sandra reached into her pocket and picked out two more stones. Would you like a pocket stone to remind you of the patience clock?"

"Yes," Kendra said, and she reached for her patience stone.

"Me too," Steven said, as he took his patience stone from her hand

"Thank you," Kendra said. She put her patience stone in her pocket.

"Thanks," Steven said. He looked at his stone for a long time, nodded, and then put it in his back pocket.

Patience: Relaxation and Directions

RELAXATION: SLOW QUIET BREATH

Focus your attention on your breath.
(pause)

Take a slow, quiet breath and exhale slowly.
(pause)

Take a slow, quiet, deep breath and exhale slowly.
(pause)

Allow your breath to become slower and deeper.
(pause)

Breathe at a pace comfortable for you.
(pause)

DIRECTIONS

Hold your patience stone in your hand. (or imagine a stone)

Be aware that you are holding a stone that is thousands of years old.

Choose a place in your life where you need patience.

When the music begins, bring patience to this place in your life and notice what happens.

MUSIC

Play *Largo from Concerti Grossi in G minor*, Op. 6, No. 8 by Corelli.
4:19 minutes

At the end of the piece of music, softly say, "The music has ended. Gently bring your awareness back to this room."

SHARING

1. Write about your experience.

    or

2. Draw your experience.

    or

3. Tell about your experience.

SUPPORT

Mark looked out the open window and saw the sun shining in a bright blue sky. He walked to the front door, opened it, and felt a warm breeze in his face.

I want to go for a walk, he thought. He called to his mom, "I'm going out for a walk."

"Have a good time," his mom said.

Mark walked out the door and headed for the woods behind his house. His footsteps made a scraping sound on the ground. Birds chattered in the treetops, and he recognized the song of a robin and a crow.

He headed toward a little stream and came to his favorite place where the water made gurgling sounds as it flowed over the rocks. He sat down by the edge of the stream, played with the stones, and even made a leaf boat that floated downstream.

When he was finished, he stood up, stretched, and walked along the stream until he came to a bridge. He paused on the bridge to watch the water swishing and swirling below him. He crossed the bridge to the other side and looked at the hill beside the path. *I wonder what's at the top of the hill.*

Mark left the path and started to climb. He had to make his own path through the bushes to climb higher. His hands reached out to push low branches out of his way to make room for his feet. Slowly he climbed higher and higher.

He paused to look up to the top of the hill. *This hill is higher than I thought. It didn't look this high when I walked on the path.* Carefully, he started to climb upward again.

Suddenly his foot slipped, and he lost his balance. He began to slide backwards down the hill. He slid faster and faster. He closed his eyes and screamed, "HELP" as loud as he could.

It felt like something strong grabbed his hand. Mark stopped sliding backwards. He opened his eyes and saw that his hand was wrapped around a branch of a big bush. He held on tightly to the strong branch.

Mark lay there on the ground clutching the branch. The bush felt friendly and he said, "Thanks. You caught me."

At that moment, Mark thought about all the people in his life who were there to help him. In his mind he saw his family, teachers at school and his neighbors.

Mark felt a big thank you coming from deep inside him. This thank you was so big that he said, "Thank you," out loud. Then he said, "Thank you," even louder; then another, "Thank you," even louder.

Mark felt strong again. He looked at the hill above him and thought, *I believe I can make it to the top.* Carefully and slowly he pulled himself up to a standing position. He put his feet on the solid earth and began to climb again. This time Mark climbed with confidence. His legs were strong, and his feet were steady. He kept his balance as he inched his way to the top.

When he reached the top, he stood tall, looked around, and said, "Wow," out loud. He could see the valley below and the road leading to his house. He pointed toward his house where his family lived. He felt a thank you, coming from deep inside of him. He thought about his family and all his friends, his teachers, and the people at school who were there to help him.

He stood tall with his feet standing firmly on the ground. He lifted up his arms toward the blue sky. He spread his fingers and shouted, "THANK YOU!"

Support: Relaxation and Directions

RELAXATION: HANDS ON HEART

Put your hands on your heart.

>*(pause)*

Take a slow breath

>*(pause)*

Take another slow quiet breath

>*(pause)*

Remember someone who has given you a helping hand

>*(pause)*

When the music begins, remember how you felt when someone gave you a helping hand.

MUSIC

Play *Barcarolle* from *Tales of Hoffman*, Op. 67, by Offenbach.
3:23 minutes

At the end of the piece of music, softly say, "The music has ended. Gently bring your awareness back to this room."

SHARING

1. Write about your experience.
   or
2. Draw your experience.
   or
3. Tell about your experience.

Trust

Sally lay with her head on her pillow and tried to go to sleep, but her eyes stayed open. She wondered, *What will it be like to go to a new school? Will I have what I need? My book bag has pencils, and paper. I even packed Snuffy. I feel better when my pink bear is with me. What if the other children see Snuffy and make fun of me?*

Sally looked over at the chair in her room and saw the outfit she had chosen to wear. *Suppose the other children make fun of my clothes. What will I do?* she wondered.

She looked at her shoes and thought, *Suppose someone laughs at my shoes?*

Sally's mother came to her room and saw she was still awake. She walked over to Sally's bed and sat down beside her. "What are you thinking about?" she asked.

"Will I have friends at my new school? Will other children laugh at me?" Sally said.

"You packed your book bag and laid out your clothes. You packed all you needed for school. You also have all that you need inside of you."

"But I did not pack anything for inside of me," Sally replied.

"You don't have to pack what is inside of you because you carry it with you all the time," her mom replied.

Sally frowned and said, "What do you mean?"

Her mother continued, "I feel your love for me. I know your heart is big because it is already packed full of love."

Sally smiled.

Her mom continued, "When you meet the girls and boys in your new school, they will be able to sense you have a big heart filled with love."

"How will they know?" Sally asked.

"They will know because of your eyes."

"Because of my eyes?"

"Yes, because of your eyes. Your eyes sparkle with the love in your heart. This love shines out of your eyes. Others will look into your eyes and feel like you can be their friend. Trust the love in your heart. Don't worry, you will make friends easily."

Sally looked up and her eyes sparkled. She gave her mother a big hug.

When her mother left her room, Sally put her hand over her heart, closed her eyes, and thought about the friends she would have at her new school.

Trust: Relaxation and Directions

RELAXATION: HEARTBEAT

Place your hand on your heart.

> *(pause)*

Breathe gently.

> *(pause)*

Breathe just a little slower.

> *(pause)*

Breathe slower and deeper.

> *(pause)*

Be aware of your heartbeat

> *(pause)*

DIRECTIONS

Be aware of the love in your heart.

When the music begins, find a way you can share that love with friends.

MUSIC

Play *Largo* from *Concerto Grossi in C major,* Op. 3, no.12, by Manfredini.
4:34 minutes

At the end of the piece of music, softly say, "The music has ended. Gently bring your awareness back to this room."

SHARING

1. Write about your experience.

    or

2. Draw your experience.

    or

3. Tell about your experience.

Access the Music Files

From the E-Book

Click the on-screen link following the specific example.

From the Print Book

Stream from the online player at LindaPowellsmi.com.

Or use the following QR Code to load the same player.

Alternatively, purchase the CD of all examples from:

StoriesMusicAndImagery.com

Stories for Older Children

Acknowledgement

Acknowledgment

Sally sat in her room looking at the books on her bookshelf and wondered, What shall I read? She pulled out a book with a raccoon, possum, and rabbit on the cover and thought, I *haven't read this book for a long time.* She took the book to her bed, lay back on her pillow, opened the book, and read out loud, "Today is the Fifth Annual Animal Beauty Pageant."

The animals gathered in a clearing in the woods. Raccoon displayed her tail so that everyone could see her beautiful stripes. She smoothed her fur so each stripe on her tail could be admired.

Sally laughed out loud and said, "That's funny. The raccoon is pampering her striped tail."

Sally turned the page and read, "The possum sat next to the raccoon and displayed her very long, slender tail." *That tail is bare. It's not very pretty,* Sally thought.

Sally turned the page and continued. "Rabbit sat beside the possum. She was hiding her tail by sitting on it."

How can the rabbit enter a beauty contest and hide her tail? She turned the page to read, "The rabbit looked at the raccoon tail with its fluffy stripes and thought, *My tail has no stripes, so it can't be as beautiful as Raccoon's tail. Possum has the longest tail I have ever seen. I have always wanted a long tail.*" She tried to fight back the tears that welled up in her eyes.

This is silly, thought Sally. *Why doesn't the rabbit realize that her little tail is beautiful too?*

Sally turned the page and read, "Here comes the judge." The picture showed the judge walking toward the contestants. He wore a dark suit, held a pen in one hand, and carried an official looking briefcase. The contestants frowned, shivered, and worried that the judge might write something bad about them.

Raccoon thought, *Maybe I didn't preen enough, and my tail stripes look crooked.*

Possum thought, *Maybe my tail isn't the longest. I didn't measure it this morning to see if it grew longer during the night.*

Rabbit was actually trembling as she thought, *I just know my tail is not good enough. It's not striped; it's not long; it's just too small.*

This book is silly, Sally thought. *Don't the animals realize that each one is beautiful in its own way? How could a judge choose just one?*

Sally yawned, closed the book and put it beside her on the bed. Her thoughts drifted back to the sleepover at Janna's house where she sat in front of a mirror with Janna and Ardis.

It all started when Janna said, "I have this cool make up. Would you like to try it?"

"Yes," Ardis said. Sally nodded.

"How do you like this color of lipstick?" Janna asked as she pulled off the cap and began to apply it to her lips.

Ardis thought, *Janna's lips are full, and mine are too small and straight. Maybe I need a lot of lipstick to make them look bigger.*

"Hand me the lipstick," Ardis said. Janna handed the lipstick to Ardis, who put some on her lips. Ardis looked into the mirror and put on more lipstick. "They still look small. I need even more lipstick." Ardis continued to put on another layer of lipstick.

Sally just sat there looking at Janna's eyes. "They are dark and big. Mine are a dull gray and look too small. Maybe I need mascara."

Sally asked, "Janna, may I use your mascara and eyebrow pencil?"

"Sure," Janna said.

Sally reached for the mascara and put it on her eyelashes. She looked into the mirror and then used the eyebrow pencil. "My eyes still look too small. I want to make them look bigger and more beautiful." She applied more color to her eyebrows.

Janna put on more rouge, and then looked in the mirror and thought, *I look pale. I don't like the color of my skin*. Janna put more rouge and powder on her face; then she added even more.

Janna's older sister, Louise, walked into the room, took one look at the girls, and tried to keep from laughing.

"Look how beautiful we are," Janna said.

"You girls had a good time playing with the makeup. You sure did use a lot of it," Louise said.

"Take our picture," requested Janna as she reached for the camera and handed it to her sister.

The girls posed for the picture. Ardis smiled her biggest smile to make her lips big. Sally opened her eyes wide to make them bigger. Janna quickly pinched her cheeks to make them look even redder.

Louise handed the camera back to Janna and said, "You girls need a lesson on how to use make up. Use just a little bit to enhance your own beauty. Don't focus on what you don't think you have. Acknowledge your own beauty."

As Louise walked toward the door she stopped to say, "Take a good look at the picture. Do you acknowledge your own beauty, or are you trying to look like someone else?"

Sally remembered what Louise said and reached for the picture. She took a closer look at the picture, and thought, *We do look like clowns with all that make up on.*

Sally laughed, put the picture back on the table beside her bed, lay back on the pillow, and yawned. She smiled as she remembered how they continued to put on even more make up after Louise left the room.

Sally yawned and then yawned another time. Her eyes closed as she thought about looking into the mirror. She was sort of dreaming about looking into the mirror, only this time it was different. In her dream Janna said, "We have to get ready for the beauty pageant. We only have a few minutes before the judge comes."

"Oh no," Sally said, "my eyes are not big enough."

"Oh no," Janna said, "my skin is too pale."

"Oh no," Ardis said, "my lips are too small."

Just then there was a knock on the door. The girls froze.

"Oh no, the judge is here, and I have not made my eyes bigger," Sally said.

"Oh no, the judge is here, and I have not made my skin look redder," Janna said.

"Oh no, the judge is here, and I have not made my lips bigger," Ardis said.

The girls gasped as the judge opened the door and walked into the room. The judge wore a dark suit, held a pen in one hand, and carried an official looking briefcase.

He opened the briefcase, took out a piece of paper, and wrote Sally on it. He looked at Sally and wrote something on the paper. The judge took out another piece of paper and wrote Janna at the top. He looked at her and wrote something. He was not smiling. He looked at Ardis, took out another piece of paper and wrote Ardis at the top. He frowned and wrote something on the paper by her name.

The judge reached into his briefcase and took out a copy of *The Only Way to Be Glamorously Beautiful*. He looked at Janna, opened the magazine to page 19, walked over to Janna, held the picture beside Janna's face, then wrote, "Not the right color."

Next the judge looked at Ardis. He opened *The Only Way to Be Glamorously Beautiful*, to page 24. He walked over to Ardis and held the picture next to her face, then wrote, "too small."

The judge looked at Sally and opened *The Only Way to Be Glamorously Beautiful* to page 36. Sally felt her mouth go dry and her knees began to shake. She looked at picture in the magazine and said, "That's not me."

She opened her mouth and shouted "Louise, Louise!" She shouted again, "Louise, Louise!"

Sally sat up in bed and looked all around her. She was alone in her room, then she realized, *I was only dreaming*. She remembered Louise saying, "Acknowledge your own beauty."

Sally picked up the picture from the sleepover and looked closely at each person and thought, *We did put on too much make up*. She put the picture down and thought about her friend Ardis. *I like the way she smiles. Her mouth turns into the warmest smile and I feel her friendship.*

Next Sally thought about Janna. *I like the way she looks at me and gives me her full attention when she talks. She has a beautiful complexion. How could the judge think my friends are not beautiful?*

Sally walked to her mirror, looked at herself and said, "I don't have to enter a beauty pageant to find out if a judge thinks I'm beautiful. I acknowledge my own beauty right now."

Acknowledgment: Relaxation and Directions

RELAXATION: BODY AWARENESS

Be aware of your feet.

> *(pause)*

Be aware of your toes.

> *(pause)*

Be aware of your heels.

> *(pause)*

Notice the place where your foot joins your ankle.

> *(pause)*

Be aware of the length of your legs.

> *(pause)*

Be aware of your hips and lower back.

> *(pause)*

Notice how long your spine is from your lower back up to your neck.

> *(pause)*

Be aware of your shoulders.

> *(pause)*

Notice how long your arms are.

> *(pause)*

Be aware of where your hands join your wrists.

> *(pause)*

Notice your fingers.

> *(pause)*

Notice the place where your neck joins your head.

(pause)

Be aware of your mouth.

(pause)

Be aware of your nose.

(pause)

Be aware of your eyes.

(pause)

Be aware of your hair.

(pause)

DIRECTIONS

Say, "I don't need a judge to tell me I'm beautiful.

I acknowledge my own beauty right now."

When the music begins, acknowledge your own beauty.

MUSIC

Play *Morning, Peer Gynt Suite #1* Op 46, by Grieg.
3:44 minutes

At the end of the piece of music, softly say, "The music has ended. Gently bring your awareness back to this room."

SHARING

1. Write about your experience.

    or

2. Draw your experience.

    or

3. Tell about your experience.

Appreciation

Jan sat in front of her mirror and frowned as she combed her hair. She thought, *I don't like my hair. It just won't do what I want it to do. Here's another tangle. Ouch!*

She turned her face sideways to get a better look at her nose. *Ugh, I don't like the way my nose looks from the side. It's too big.*

Then she saw it—a zit. *Yuck, how could my face do this to me? It's nasty.*

Jan stood up to get a full-length view of herself. *Oh no, did I gain another pound . . . in the wrong place?* She stepped forward and said aloud, "I don't like what I see in this mirror."

At that moment something happened, and it was not like Jan moved closer to the mirror. Instead, it was like she stepped forward, went through the mirror, and saw herself in a mirror behind the first one.

"What happened?" Jan asked as she stepped back and looked into the first mirror again. She saw her unruly hair, her long nose, the nasty zit, and that extra pound in the wrong place.

Hmmm, that was weird. She glanced at the clock, then reached for her clothes to get dressed for school.

Later that day, Jan came back to her room. She put her book bag on the floor by her desk and hung her jacket in her closet.

She looked at the mirror and frowned. She walked closer to the mirror and looked at her hair. More strands were out of place. Her nose was still long. Her zit looked even bigger. She looked at her body and thought, *Maybe, that extra pound makes me look more mature. I want to take a closer look.*

She stepped forward and then suddenly she was looking into the mirror behind the first one. "Now you are honoring your body," were the words she heard as she looked into the second mirror.

Jan was so surprised that she jumped back. *Did this really happen?* she wondered.

Jan looked into the first mirror and saw her unruly hair, long nose, zit, and body. *I'll try this again*, she thought.

She turned her head to the side and said, "Maybe my nose isn't so bad after all."

She stepped forward and sure enough there was the second mirror behind the first. She heard the words, "Your nose is beautiful because it is your nose."

Jan smiled and stepped back. Maybe this will work for my hair too. She said, "My hair can be beautiful even if it is out of place."

She stepped forward to the second mirror and heard, "Your hair is beautiful; you can choose how to wear your hair in beauty."

Jan smiled and stepped backwards.

Oh, what about this awful zit? How can this be a good thing? she wondered.

Jan stepped forward to the second mirror. She saw that the zit was still there, but it was changing. It was getting smaller in size, and it was like it was going away. "All parts of you can heal," were the words she heard before she stepped backwards again.

I like this second mirror, thought Jan.

The next morning Jan looked into the mirror. She almost started to criticize how she looked; then she remembered the second mirror.

When she stepped forward and saw herself in the second mirror, she felt different about herself.

Jan stepped backward and looked at the first mirror and wanted to say, "I don't like the way I look. Why can't my hair be like that model I saw in the glamour magazine?"

She paused and realized, *I can say positive words, or I can complain about what I don't like about the way I look.*

Jan stepped forward and looked into the second mirror. Something changed inside. She felt like looking at herself and saying, "I love you, Jan, just the way you are."

Jan stepped back and wanted to argue, *But I don't like the way I look.* She frowned, then realized, *This is an unkind way to feel. I want to change.*

So, she stepped forward to see herself in the second mirror. She heard the words, "Love yourself. Appreciate yourself. Honor who you are from the inside out."

She stepped back to see herself in the first mirror. She took a new look at herself and smiled.

When Jan stepped forward to see herself in the second mirror, she heard these words, "When you love yourself, you have a positive attitude about yourself. It is your choice. You can criticize and not like yourself, or you can look into this second mirror of love and appreciation."

Jan stepped back from the mirror and thought, *I do have a choice to love and accept myself, or to criticize myself. It's my choice. I choose the second mirror. I choose to love and appreciate myself.*

Appreciation: Relaxation and Directions

RELAXATION: TENSE AND RELEASE

Find a comfortable position for your body.

Allow your body to become quiet.

(pause)

Tighten the muscles of one leg as you raise it a few inches off the floor.

(pause)

Let go of the tension as you allow the leg to relax and gently touch the floor.

(pause)

Notice how the muscles of that leg feel now.

(pause)

Tighten the muscles of other leg as you raise it a few inches off the floor.

(pause)

Let go of the tension as you allow the leg to relax and gently touch the floor.

(pause)

Notice how the muscles of that leg feel now.

(pause)

Now tighten the muscles of your stomach and hold.

(pause)

Let go of the tension as you allow the muscles to be soft and relaxed.

(pause)

Raise your shoulders up toward your ears and hold.

    (pause)

Let go of the tension as you allow the muscles to be soft and relaxed.

    (pause)

Now make a fist with one hand and hold.

    (pause)

Let go of the tension as you allow the muscles of your hand and arm to be soft and relaxed.

    (pause)

Now make a fist with the other hand and hold.

    (pause)

Let go of the tension as you allow the muscles of your hand and arm to be soft and relaxed.

    (pause)

Clench your teeth together and hold.

    (pause)

Let go of the tension as you allow the muscles of your jaw to be soft and relaxed.

    (pause)

Squint your eyes and hold.

    (pause)

Let go of the tension as you allow the muscles to be soft and relaxed.

STORIES, MUSIC, AND IMAGERY PROCESS

DIRECTIONS

Imagine a first mirror in front of you.

(pause)

Look in the mirror and notice what you see.

(pause)

When the music begins, imagine leaning forward to see into a second mirror of appreciation. Notice what you see.

(pause)

MUSIC

Play *Intermezzo from Cavalleria Rusticana* by Mascagni.
3:59 minutes.

At the end of the piece of music, softly say, "The music has ended. Gently bring your awareness back to this room."

SHARING

1. Write about your experience.

or

2. Draw your experience.

or

3. Tell about your experience.

Choice

CHOICE

Charles was supposed to be in bed...asleep. Instead, he was playing his favorite game. *I'll just play a little longer*, he thought.

The clock ticked and kept ticking. Charles yawned and finally looked at the clock. *Uh oh, it's later than I thought.* He yawned again, put his game on the table, and yawned one more time.

Charles lay back on his pillow and imagined going to his favorite store to get a new game. *What will it be?* he wondered.

He drifted from a daydream into a sleeping dream where he saw a salesman wearing a strange looking hat that had many bold zigzag colors all over it. Charles walked over to the counter and said, "I didn't know you were allowed to wear a weird hat to work."

The salesman with the multicolored hat said, "It is my choice." Charles looked into the man's eyes and saw a twinkle there.

"Which game do you want to play?" the man asked, as he looked directly at Charles.

"Oh, I don't care. Any game will do," Charles answered.

The man asked again, "Which one do you choose?"

"I don't care. Just give me one," Charles replied.

"You do have a choice," said the man at the counter, as he looked at Charles.

Charles just stood there and said nothing. When he looked up at the man, he noticed that the man had a different hat on his head. This one had colorful sequins on the top and was surrounded by bells dangling all around the edges.

"I didn't know you were allowed to wear a funny hat to work, either," Charles said.

"It is my choice," the man said. "Do you want the game?"

"Yes, just give me any game," Charles answered.

"It is your choice," said the man behind the counter, as he reached for a game and handed it to Charles.

Charles took the game and pressed the start button. There on the screen was someone in his class laughing at him.

I don't think I'll like this game, thought Charles. *I'm afraid someone else will laugh at me.* The screen changed, and he saw his best friend laughing at him. Soon everyone was laughing at him.

Charles turned off the game and handed it back to the man at the counter. "I want to return this game. I don't like being laughed at."

The man took the game, and Charles saw the man now wore a hat that had a pair of boxing gloves on the top of the hat. "How about a game called 'Hit and Yell'?" the man asked.

"OK," Charles said. The man handed him the game. Charles pressed the start button, looked at the screen, and saw himself on the playground facing a big, mean bully. Charles made a fist and was ready to fight. The bully hit first, and Charles noticed the teacher looking at him and he yelled, "But he hit me first, so I have to hit him back." Suddenly a punch came from the other side of the screen.

Charles turned the game off, handed it back to the man and said, "I don't like this game, and I don't want it."

"It is your choice. You can step out of a game and choose something different," said the man with the sparkling eyes.

Charles saw the man was now wearing a baseball cap.

"I didn't know you were allowed to wear a baseball cap to work," Charles said.

"It is my choice," the man said. "I choose to play a good game of baseball. I choose to do my best and play a fair game."

Charles looked at the games in front of him and asked, "Which is a good game for me."

"It is your choice," the man said. This time he had a different hat on his head. It was a graduation cap.

"I didn't know you could wear a graduation cap to work," Charles said.

"It is my choice," the man said. "I choose to study and learn so I can play the game of graduation."

Charles looked down at the games and asked, "What's this one?" as he pointed to another game.

Charles looked up and saw the man was wearing a hat with two children on the top. They were shaking hands. Below the hands was the word *Friendship* in big green letters.

Charles read the words and thought, *But how do I know if someone will laugh at me, or hit me, or yell at me?*

"It is your choice," the man said.

"What do you mean it is my choice? I can't control others."

"It is your choice to control you," was the man's answer.

"What do you mean?" Charles asked.

"If you are afraid of being hit, and think about it often, then you can draw it to you," the man said. Charles picked up the game and pressed start.

Charles looked and saw a big tough guy making a fist. Next to him was someone with his hand out as if to shake hands.

"Oh, I get it, I can choose to hit or shake hands," Charles said.

"It is your choice," the man said. "What you choose is what you get. When you walk out on the playground, do you look around to see if someone is waiting to hit you or do you look around with eyes of friendship? What you choose to think in your head is like wearing a hat that others can see."

"A hat that others can see?" Charles asked. He frowned. "Do you mean that what I think is like wearing a hat?"

"Yes," said the man holding the friendship game. "Can you tell if someone else wants to be a friend?"

"Yes, I can tell by the way they walk and talk," Charles answered.

"Others can tell by the way you walk and talk. Walk away from someone who might hit. Look around and choose to be friendly. Others will want to be your friend."

Charles looked up and saw a different hat on the man's head. The words on the hat read, "Choose what game you will play."

"Choose what game you will play," were the words Charles heard in his head when his alarm went off the next morning.

I can choose what game I play, thought Charles as he got up and stared at himself in the mirror. He smiled and said aloud, "I choose the game of friendship."

Choice: Relaxation and Directions

RELAXATION: HANDS ON HEART

Place your hands on your heart.

> *(pause)*

Breathe gently.

> *(pause)*

Breathe just a little slower.

> *(pause)*

As you breathe more slowly, focus on your heart.

DIRECTIONS

Imagine it is time to go to the playground. Be aware of how you feel. What kind of hat would you wear that reflects who you are?

MUSIC

Play *Animato* from *Symphony No. 1* by Still.

3.16 minutes

At the end of the piece of music, softly say, "The music has ended. Gently bring your awareness back to this room."

SHARING

1. Write about your experience.
   > *or*
2. Draw your experience.
   > *or*
3. Tell about your experience.

Communication

"He won't listen to me. My brother just won't listen to me," Dana complained as she sat down at the kitchen table. She folded her arms, looked at her mom and said, "He acts like he didn't even hear a word I said. He's so stupid."

"Do you want him to listen or to agree with you?" her mom asked.

Dana pressed her lips together. She did not answer.

"Communication is about listening and sharing," her mom explained.

"Suppose he won't listen back?" Dana asked.

"When he doesn't think you heard him, he might be just as frustrated as you. Sometimes it helps to pause and take a breath. During that little pause, focus on what the other person is really saying."

Dana frowned, shook her head, then asked, "How do I know what they are really saying?"

"Listen to what they are saying, not what you want them to say," her mother responded. "When it is your turn, you can share what you really want to share from your heart."

Dana nodded as if she understood what her mom was saying.

"When you listen and share from your heart," her mom said, "there is a real exchange of communication. Take some time to explore what this means for you. Go be with yourself."

Dana walked out the door and into the back yard toward the path in the woods. She remembered her mother's words, "Listen to what they are saying, not what you want them to say. When it is your turn, you can share what you really want to share from your heart."

Dana wondered, *How do I know which is which?*

She remembered her bus ride to school that morning. *Jason came over and sat beside me and asked to copy my homework. He's so cute; I really want him to like me. I said yes, and he copied my homework. When he finished, he just handed my homework back to me and went to sit with his friends. He didn't even say thank you. That didn't feel like communication.*

Dana walked slowly and looked up when she heard a bird singing. She saw a song sparrow sitting on a branch of the tree. It opened its beak to sing again. Another sparrow answered from a nearby tree. *Maybe the birds know how to communicate.*

Dana walked down the path to her favorite sitting place under a tall poplar tree. *How can I speak from my heart?* she wondered. She leaned back against the strong trunk and closed her eyes.

She imagined she was walking along a path in the woods. The woods were like the one where she sat, except somehow different. There was a fork in the path. *Hmm, I could go to the left, or I could go to the right. Which path should I choose?*

She looked down the fork on the left and saw a sign. *That's strange. It looks like there is a street sign on the path. I wonder what it says.*

Dana imagined walking over to the sign to take a closer look. She read the words, "You are 'right' when you take this path."

I want to be right, thought Dana as she walked down the fork to the left.

Suddenly she saw another sign. She walked fast until she was close enough to read the words, "You will be popular when you walk this path."

Of course, I want to be popular. I want the other girls and the cute boys to like me. This is the path I want. As she walked along, there were no birds singing.

I see another sign. I wonder what it says, thought Dana as she hurried down the path. She tripped and almost fell over a dead branch in her path. She stopped and looked around. The leaves on the bushes were dry and brittle.

Her feet made crunchy sounds as she walked through dead leaves. The next sign had the words, "You will get what you want when you follow this path."

Dana shivered as a chilly gust of wind blew across her face. She frowned and thought, *I'm not quite sure about this path. Maybe I will read just one more sign. I can get to it if I can just push these branches away.*

Dana forced her way through the debris and read, "You will win every argument."

Dana stopped and remembered what her mom had said, "Communication is not about winning an argument. Communication is about sharing from my heart."

"I don't want to follow this path," Dana said, and she turned around and started to walk back toward the fork in the path. She stepped over dead branches and saw the back of the sign she had just passed. It said, "Your way is best. Don't listen to what someone else says." Dana shook her head as she walked a little faster. She read the back of the next sign that said, "Don't you want to have your way?"

Dana shook her head and ran past the back of the next sign without even reading it. Finally, she returned to the fork in the path. Dana gave a sigh of relief and looked at the other path.

Where does this one go? she wondered, as she stepped forward on the new path. She smiled when she heard a bird twittering and looked up into the tree and saw several birds. They spread their wings and flew together toward a nearby tree.

Dana heard a rustling in the tree and looked up to see two squirrels playing as they chased each other up and down the trunk of the tree, ran out on a branch of the tree, and leaped gracefully to the next tree.

Bushes with green leaves grew beside the wide path through the woods, and the sound of bubbling water of a stream filled the air. Dana walked to a quiet pool of clear water and sat down. She looked at her reflection as she leaned over the water. I'm smiling back at myself.

Suddenly Dana saw another face in the pool of water. The face was surrounded by flowing hair and had clear eyes and a warm smile. Dana heard soft words, "Look how the water is moving in the stream. Communication can flow just like water in this stream. What happens when you put a leaf into the stream?"

Dana reached for a leaf that reminded her of a yellow boat; she put it into the stream. It bobbed up and down as it was carried along by the gentle flowing water. It went around a rock, over a mini waterfall, and on down the stream.

Dana looked back to the pretty face in the water and heard, "Allow words from your heart to flow and carry you forward as you communicate."

Dana opened her eyes and looked up at the branches of the tall poplar tree above her. She took a deep breath and thought about the two choices at the fork in the path. The first path was dark where the selfish me walked. The second path is beautiful. I choose to walk the path of my heart.

Communication: Relaxation and Directions

RELAXATION: HEARTBEAT

Focus on the beat of your heart.

> *(pause)*

Feel the beat of your heart deep inside you.

> *(pause)*

Notice how fast or slow your heart is beating.

> *(pause)*

DIRECTIONS

Imagine you are in the woods and you see two paths.

Notice what each path looks like.

Notice what is around the paths.

When the music begins, choose which path you will walk.

MUSIC

Play *Minuet* by Boccherini.
4:27 minutes

At the end of the piece of music, softly say: "The music has ended. Gently bring your awareness back to this room."

SHARING

1. Write about your experience.

>   *or*

2. Draw your experience.

>   *or*

3. Tell about your experience.

Expression

Sam ran as fast as he could toward the soccer ball, but it rolled right past him. A tall player from the other team kicked the ball and scored the final point of the game. "We lost, 3 to 2," murmured Sam. He looked at the ground as he passed the other team members and avoided looking at the coach as he left the field. His shoulders drooped forward as he walked toward the car where his father waited to pick him up.

"What happened?" his dad asked. "You look disappointed."

"I'm not good enough," blurted Sam.

"Why do you think you are not good enough?" his dad asked.

"We lost and it was my fault," Sam answered.

"Does one game mean you're not good enough?" his dad asked.

"Well . . . it feels like it," Sam said in a weak voice.

"You sound like you're caught on the roller coaster of competition," his dad said.

"What do you mean?"

"Competition is like a roller coaster; sometimes you are at the top, and sometimes you are at the bottom. You feel better than everyone else when you are on the top. You feel less than others when you are at the bottom," his dad explained.

"I'm at the bottom now and I feel bad," Sam said.

"You have a choice. You can ride on the roller coaster of competition or you can be who you are and express yourself through the game."

Sam frowned and asked, "What do you mean?"

"Let me tell you a story," his dad said.

Once there was a kingdom that had two castles. One castle flew a flag that had stripes going up and down, and the other castle flew a flag that had circles on it. Some people thought their flag with stripes was the best; the other people thought their flag with circles was better. So, they decided to have a contest to see which one was the best.

People from the castle that flew the flag with stripes wore striped shirts, striped jewelry, and hats with stripes going up and down. People from the castle that flew the flag with circles wore clothes decorated with circles, round bracelets, and round hats. It was easy to see who was from which castle.

Competition day began with a parade of the athletes. Only the best athletes made it through all the tryouts and were chosen to be the best runners, jumpers, throwers, climbers, and swimmers. When the parade began, the athletes held their heads high and flexed their strong muscles.

When the games started, people cheered when someone won an event. The winner strutted around with raised arms, as if to say, "I'm better than all the others."

On a hill overlooking the games sat a man dressed in a green robe. Beside him was a lady wearing a long green gown. Both sat quietly watching, listening, and waiting. It was not long before an athlete stumbled up the hill toward them.

He was crying and wailed, "I lost the game. I'm not good enough. All the people cheered for the winner. I left and was not able to hold back my tears."

"Come sit by us," said the man in the green robe. "Look at the games from this hill and tell me what you see."

"I see the people sitting in the stands. Each person is cheering for their team. I see some athletes winning and some losing," the athlete said.

"Yes," said the man in the robe. "Now even look closer. What do you see?"

"I see the winner strutting around with his arms up while people cheer. I see the loser walking away with his shoulders slumped. He looks like he is crying too."

"What happened last year at the games?" asked the man in the green robe.

Suddenly the picture shifted to the year before. There were people in the stands cheering for the winner. The loser walked away with shoulders drooping forward and head down. The picture shifted again to the year before that, and the year before that. Each time it looked the same.

"Year after year, it is the same scene," explained the lady in the green robe. "Sometimes one castle has the best athletes, the next year the other castle has the best athletes. Who is the winner?"

The athlete shook his head and answered, "Neither one really. Sometimes they are the best, and sometimes they lose. What is the point of the games?"

"Ah, that is a good question," said the lady in the green gown. "Look on the other side of the hill. What do you see?"

"Where?"

"Over there." The man and woman pointed to the other side of the hill.

"I see another kingdom with people in it. I never knew this kingdom was there," the athlete said. "I worked so hard to be the best, that I never explored the other side of the hill."

"Look closely and tell me what you see," the lady said.

"There's only one castle. I see people planting a garden together. Several are taking care of farm animals. I see a group of people swimming in the lake. The people are smiling and laughing."

"Are there any races?" asked the man in the robe.

"Yes, I see two boys racing. One won and the other one is patting him on the back and giving him a compliment."

"They celebrate each person," explained the lady. "In this kingdom, the people express their talents. They are growing and having fun in the process. Look at their faces."

"They look happy and peaceful. Some are even singing," exclaimed the athlete. "How can the people be so happy?"

"They do not live by the flags of better than or less than. They are not on the competition roller coaster. They have another way to live," explained the man in the green robe.

"What is that way?" the athlete asked.

"The people are free to be," the lady said.

"What do you mean free to be? Be what?" the athlete asked.

"Free to express who they are without judging themselves and others as better than or less then."

The man continued, "Look at the school. They are learning for the joy of learning; not to get the highest grades or the most gold stars. They can express their talents without having to be better than any other person. They accept who they are. This is why they are free to be who they are. When being is more important than doing, everyone shines because each person has something to offer. Each person is cheered for who they are," the man said.

Sam frowned when his dad finished the story. Sam thought about the story, then said, "That all sounds good in a fairy tale, but I live in the land of the castles and competition."

"Yes, I understand, and soccer is still about playing well, playing fairly, enjoying yourself as you express who you really are."

Sam nodded.

His dad continued, "Even though there's competition in the world, you still have a choice of which side of the hill you are on. Your thoughts and attitude determine if you choose being or judging. You can still focus on accepting who you are and expressing yourself in whatever you are involved in now. It could be through studying, running, dancing, or playing basketball."

Sam smiled, and his dad continued. "Even when you are playing competitive sports, you can be in a centered place. This land of peace is inside you."

"I get it," Sam said. "If I want to be better than someone else, I'm on the competition roller coaster. If I'm learning and expressing my talents, I'm being me and accepting me."

"You got it," his dad said.

Expression: Relaxation and Direction

RELAXATION: TENSE AND RELEASE LONG

Find a comfortable position for your body.

Allow your body to become quiet.

Tighten the muscles of one leg as you raise it a few inches off the floor.

(pause)

Let go of the tension as you allow the leg to relax and gently touch the floor.

(pause)

Notice how the muscles of that leg feel now.

(pause)

Tighten the muscles of other leg as you raise it a few inches off the floor.

(pause)

Let go of the tension as you allow the leg to relax and gently touch the floor.

(pause)

Notice how the muscles of that leg feel now.

(pause)

Now tighten the muscles of your stomach and hold.

(pause)

Let go of the tension as you allow the muscles to be soft and relaxed.

(pause)

Raise your shoulders up toward your ears and hold.

(pause)

Let go of the tension as you allow the muscles to be soft and relaxed.

(pause)

Now make a fist with one hand and hold.

(pause)

Let go of the tension as you allow the muscles of your hand and arm to be soft and relaxed.

(pause)

Now make a fist with the other hand and hold.

(pause)

Let go of the tension as you allow the muscles of your hand and arm to be soft and relaxed.

(pause)

Clench your teeth together and hold.

(pause)

Let go of the tension as you allow the muscles of your jaw to be soft and relaxed.

(pause)

Squint your eyes and hold.

(pause)

Let go of the tension as you allow the muscles to be soft and relaxed.

DIRECTIONS

Remember a time when you were on the roller coaster of competition. It could be a feeling of better than or less than.

Notice how it feels.

When the music begins, imagine getting off the roller coaster of competition. Focus on your character education quality of "being" that you could express.

MUSIC

Play *Canon* by Pachelbel.
4:45 minutes

At the end of the piece of music, softly say:

"The music has ended.

"Gently bring your awareness back to this room."

SHARING

1. Write about your experience.

   or

2. Draw your experience.

   or

3. Tell about your experience.

Focus

Donald sat at his desk in school, yawned, and thought, *I know I will be bored today.*

"Today we will learn about air currents. Open your science books and read pages 84 to 86," instructed his teacher.

Donald got out his book, opened it, and started to read about the wind. When he looked at the picture of the air currents, his thoughts took off on the wind, and he fantacized flying his own plane. He moved the control stick to the right, and the plane turned to the right. He made the plane soar above the trees and up over the hills. Ahead was a mountain, and he flew the plane up, up, and up even higher . . .

"Does anyone need more time?" the teacher asked.

Donald blinked and raised his hand. He looked around the room, and only two other students had their hands up.

Donald quickly tried to scan the rest of the reading assignment. It was too long, and he couldn't finish.

"Answer the questions I'm writing on the board," the teacher said.

Donald looked at the first question. *I don't know the answer*, thought Donald. *I'll have to make up an answer.*

A few minutes later the teacher said, "It's time to collect the papers."

Tim sat at the desk beside Donald and was the first one to hand in his paper. He looked at Donald and smirked.

Donald put his pencil down. He had two unanswered questions. He handed his paper to the teacher. Neither he nor the teacher smiled.

Donald looked over at Tim and thought, *He always gets an 'A' in this class. I'll show him.*

Donald fantasized that he and Tim had swords. Tim swung his sword first and Donald blocked the blow. They both stepped back. Tim advanced again. Donald countered the attack and swung his sword. With a mighty whack, he knocked Tim's sword out of his hand.

"Your hand is waving in the air. Do you have a question?" the teacher asked.

Donald looked at his teacher with a blank expression on his face. He shook his head no and put his hand down.

"It is time to choose your topic for your science project," the teacher said. "Write down some ideas for your outline."

When the bell rang, Donald was the first one out of the room. As he walked down the crowded hallway, he looked around and thought, *I'm short. The girls are taller than I am. I'm even shorter than most of the boys in my class. I wish I were tall and had muscles that flexed big and strong.*

Donald pretended he was in a gym lifting weights. His muscles were strong, and he could lift the biggest weights. He could even lift the biggest weight over his head.

"Hey Donald, where are you going?" Keith asked. "You just passed your classroom. Why are you holding your books over your head?"

Donald brought his attention back to the hallway, and put his books under his arm. He turned around without answering Keith's question, and walked back to his classroom.

"Today is our midterm exam," the teacher said. "I hope all of you have studied the material."

What exam? Donald wondered. *I don't remember anything about an exam.*

The teacher handed out the exam papers and said, "Write your name at the top of the page. Begin your test now."

Donald pretended to be Professor Eruditis, who wore a graduation robe and tasseled hat. Donald thought to himself, Professor Eruditis can answer any question on this paper. Donald wrote something for every question as quickly as he could.

The teacher came around to collect the test papers. She picked up Donald's paper, looked at it, frowned, and said, "Your name is not Professor 'Eru' something. Write your real name on the paper." She handed the paper back and stood there until Donald wrote his name and handed the paper back to her. The look on her face made everyone in the class laugh.

Donald scrunched down in his desk and tried to make the color of his cheeks look normal instead of bright red. Tim sat across the room and pointed to Donald's cheeks and laughed out loud.

It seemed like an eternity before the dismissal bell rang. Donald ran out of the school and started to gallop. Donald pretended to ride a big white horse. He yelled "giddy up," and his white horse galloped faster and faster.

His little sister stood in the doorway, laughed, and asked, "Why are you galloping up to the front door?"

"You wouldn't understand," snapped Donald, as he dismounted and walked up the front steps into the living room.

"How was your day in school?" his mom asked.

"Same as usual—boring—each class is boring, and the teachers don't understand me," Donald answered. He quickly walked past his mom and went to his room and closed the door.

"Nobody understands me," he moaned as he sat in his chair.

His mom came to his door and asked, "Are you doing your homework?"

"Yeah, yeah," Donald answered as he pulled his science book out of his book bag.

Why do I have to do this stupid assignment? Donald wondered as he pulled out his desk chair and sat in it. His body was at his desk, but his attention was focused on his trip over the trees in his hot-air balloon. He could see the river and the mountains ahead. Beyond the mountains was the ocean. He traveled over the ocean to the distant countries.

Just then his mom knocked on the door and asked, "May I come in?"

"Yes," Donald said as he brought his attention back to the room.

"I just received a call from your teacher."

"Oh no," Donald said. "What did she say?"

"She said you were not paying attention in class and missed the lesson she taught."

"Well, I was in class," argued Donald.

"Just sitting in class is not the same as being fully present," his mom said.

She looked into Donald's eyes. Then she looked at his empty paper on his desk and said, "You have been working on your homework for thirty minutes and there's nothing written on your paper. How come?"

"The homework is boring and . . . "

"Where were you when you were supposed to be doing your homework?" his mom asked.

"I was sitting at my desk holding my pencil," Donald answered.

"That is where your physical body was sitting. Where were your thoughts?" his mom asked.

"I was pretending I was in a hot air balloon gliding over the river," Donald answered.

"So, your body was in the now, and your thoughts were floating off someplace else. What does that mean?" she asked.

"I guess that means all parts of me are not working together."

"What happens as a result?" his mom asked.

Donald frowned and thought, *I really don't want to answer that question.* Instead, Donald asked a question, "But isn't imagination important?"

"Definitely," his mom said. "Scientists like Einstein used tons of imagination their work."

Donald nodded his head.

His mother continued, "Imagination is creative, but fantasizing separates you from the moment, and can even be used to avoid something you don't want to do."

Uh oh, thought Donald as he remembered his fantasy of lifting a heavy barbell. *No wonder Keith laughed at me when I walked past the door to my classroom with my books high above my head.*

Donald looked at his mom and said, "I understand." He paused, then asked, "What can I do when I'm bored in class?"

"Are you bored because you don't want to do something? Give me an example," requested his mom.

"I had this assignment to read in science class, and I had only read a few paragraphs when the teacher told us to answer questions about it."

"Did you fantasize instead of reading it?" his mom asked.

"Well, I guess I did. The assignment was about air currents. I pretended I was flying a plane and..."

"Perfect example," interrupted his mom. "You didn't like to do the reading assignment, so you fantasized about flying the plane to make yourself feel better. The fantasy kept you from doing your class work. Your body was in class, but your fantasy separated your thoughts. That's where you lose your power of concentration."

Lose my power? Donald thought, as he remembered his cheeks getting red when the teacher made him write is real name on the test paper.

"I'm not sure I understand," Donald said.

"Where can you use your imagination in a creative way?" his mom asked.

"I don't know." Donald paused, then said, "Well, we do have a science project to do before the end the month."

"That would be a perfect place to use your imagination to help you find new ideas of how to do your project."

"Maybe I could choose air currents as my topic. I could make this plane and show how the pilot steers the plane through different kinds of air currents," Donald said with enthusiasm in his voice. "Maybe I could include how air currents affect different size airplanes."

"Great ideas," his mom said. "This could be a good science project. Collect your ideas together and expand them into your project."

Donald continued, "I could even include how head winds and tail winds affect the amount of fuel that is used."

"You're using your imagination to bring new ideas into the present moment. NOW you are fully present in the NOW," observed his mom.

His mom looked over at the empty homework paper on the desk and asked, "When do you want start?"

"NOW I can start my homework," Donald suggested.

His mom smiled and said, "NOW you are fully in the NOW," and NOW is a great time to start."

Both Donald and his mom laughed together.

Focus: Relaxation and Directions

RELAXATION: COUNTING BACKWARDS FROM 10 TO 1

We will count backwards from 10 to 1.

Begin with 10 as you notice how your body feels.

(pause)

Allow your body to relax as I say 9.

(pause)

Allow your body to become very quiet as I say 8.

(pause)

Let go of some tension as I say 7.

(pause)

Find a way to be even quieter as I say 6.

(pause)

Let go of some more tension as I say 5.

(pause)

Relax even more as I say 4.

(pause)

Your body is even more quiet as I say 3.

(pause)

You can be even more relaxed as I say 2.

(pause)

Feel your body even more relaxed as I say 1.

(pause)

DIRECTIONS

Remember a time when you focused your attention and completed a task or project.

What did you focus on?

MUSIC

Play *Rondo: Allegro* from *Cello Concerto in D major* by Haydn.
4:41 minutes

At the end of the piece of music, softly say, "The music has ended. Gently bring your awareness back to this room."

SHARING

1. Write about your experience.

   or

2. Draw your experience.

   or

3. Tell about your experience.

GRATITUDE

Sam looked out his window and saw the bright sunlight filtering down through the trees. Shadows danced on the ground as a slight breeze made the branches sway.

I want to be outside. He opened the door and walked outside into the warm breeze. The sunlight made his hair shine as he skipped along the driveway.

Sam stopped when he heard a bird sing, *"Cheerilee, cheeriup!"* He looked up into the tree and saw a robin with its beak open and its chest puffed up as it sang its full-bodied song. He turned his head when he heard *"Teekettie teekettie!"* and saw a smaller brown bird with its tail pointed up toward the sky. *I see you, Wren. You have a big song coming out of such a small beak. Thank you for your beautiful songs.*

Sam walked along the garden and realized, *The flowers are red, orange, yellow, green, blue, indigo, and violet. It's like a rainbow growing on the ground.*

"Thank you, trees. Thank you, sun. Thank you, birds. Thank you, flowers. Thank you, wonderful world," he sang, as he danced in the beauty of nature.

"Time for breakfast!" Sam heard his mother call through the open kitchen window.

Sam ran to the front door, opened it, and sniffed. "I love pancakes," he shouted as he bounced into the kitchen.

"You look happy this morning," his mother said.

"It's beautiful outside. The birds are singing, the sun is shining, and the flowers are all the colors of the rainbow."

"I'm glad you have gratitude for the beauty of nature," his mom said.

"Gratitude?" Sam asked.

"Gratitude is appreciating something, feeling it deep inside, and then showing it on the outside," his mom answered.

"I even said, 'Thank you' out loud," Sam said.

"You experienced gratitude," his mom confirmed.

"Thank you for breakfast," Sam said.

"You're welcome," his mother said. "A big breakfast will give you the energy you need for your baseball game. Your carpool will be here in five minutes."

Sam put water and a snack into his backpack, and headed toward the door.

Later that day, Sam walked back into the house. His head was hanging low, his shoulders drooped, and he was not smiling. His mother took one look at Sam and said, "You look sad. Did something happen at the baseball game?"

"I did something stupid . . . absolutely stupid. I should have known better, but I did it anyway," Sam wailed. "Then, someone on my team called me stupid in front of everybody. I know I messed up big time, but he didn't have to say it so everyone could hear it. We lost because of me."

"Are you blaming yourself for losing the whole game?" his mother gently asked.

"Yes, it was all my fault. I threw the ball to second base and forgot to check on the person who ran home and scored the winning point."

"Do you know you can feel gratitude in this situation?" his mom asked.

"No way," yelled Sam. "I made an awful mistake, and everyone is mad at me. Only the other team could be grateful for my stupid mistake that let them win," yelled Sam, as tears streamed down his face.

"Can you still be grateful for yourself?" his mom asked.

"How could I possibly be grateful for myself? I messed everything up. I just wish I could start the game all over. I wouldn't make that mistake again."

"Now that's something to be grateful for," his mom suggested.

"What do you mean?"

"It sounds like you learned a big lesson. You learned what not to do. Now you know what to do the next time. You can feel gratitude."

"I still don't get it," Sam said.

"You had the opportunity to learn what does not work. You recognized it. The next time you will make other choices," his mom explained.

Sam sniffled and looked at his mom.

"You can either tear yourself down by calling yourself stupid, or you can learn a lesson. Gratitude can help you grow into a better ball player," his mom said.

"I think I understand," Sam said as he dried his eyes.

The next day, Sam walked to the park to meet his friends. He walked over and looked directly at them, and said, "I want to play and I won't make the same mistake. I'm ready for a new game."

His friends smiled. "That's OK," they said.

"We'll let it slide this time," teased one of his friends. They all laughed and walked to the baseball field together.

Gratitude: Relaxation and Directions

RELAXATION: BREATHE SLOWLY AND DEEPLY

Take a quiet, deep breath and exhale slowly.

(pause)

Take another slow, quiet, deep breath and exhale slowly.

(pause)

Continue to breathe slowly and deeply.

(pause)

Be aware of your slow, quiet breath.

(pause)

DIRECTIONS

Remember a time when you made a mistake.

When the music begins, look deeper to find something you learned for which you can be grateful.

MUSIC

Play *Legend – Moderato from Serenade for Strings in E major*, Op. 22 by Dvorak.

4:13 minutes

At the end of the piece of music, softly say, "The music has ended. Gently bring your awareness back to this room."

SHARING

1. Write about your experience.

    or

2. Draw your experience.

    or

3. Tell about your experience.

Persistence

Christine sat at her desk at school and listened to her teacher say, "I'm returning the first draft of your writing assignment. Corrections and suggestions are in red. Your job is to make the corrections and add the suggestions to your writing."

Christine looked at her paper and frowned. The corners of her mouth turned downward as she stared at all the red marks. *How can I correct all of these mistakes?* she wondered. She folded one arm over the other and just sat there looking at her paper.

The teacher walked by and asked, "What's the matter? Are you stuck?"

Christine looked up and said, "This is too hard; I just can't do it. I did it once, and now there are all these corrections. It's like I have to do it all over again."

"You wrote the rough draft, and now you can improve it by following the suggestions on your paper. I understand that this is a hard assignment, but it's not too hard for you. With persistence, you will be able to finish the assignment," the teacher suggested.

Christine just sat there with her arms folded. At the end of class, the teacher said, "Your homework is to finish making the corrections on your paper."

Christine put the paper into her book bag and walked out of the room. Later that afternoon, Christine sat down to do her homework. She put the writing assignment on the table, frowned, folded her arms, and just stared at the red marks.

Her mother walked into her room and asked, "What's your homework?"

"This writing assignment. Look at all the red marks I have to correct. It's too hard for me. I'll never be able to do it," Christine complained.

"I believe you have enough persistence to finish the paper," her mother said.

"There's that word again. I don't even know what it means."

"Here's an example," her mom said. "When you were a baby you were determined to walk. You pulled yourself up at a table and bounced to get your leg muscles stronger. Then you let go of the table and stood all by yourself. It was not long before you took your first step. Now look at you. You run and dance with ease. You stayed with it until you could do it. That's persistence."

Her mother gave Christine a hug before she walked out of the room. She turned and said, "I know you can use persistence to finish your homework."

Christine stared at her paper and thought, *This assignment is much harder than walking.* She folded her arms again and just sat there.

"Hi, Sis," her brother said as he walked by her room. "Why are you just sitting at your desk doing nothing?"

"This assignment is too hard for me and I can't do it," Christine answered.

"It's only too hard if you think it is," responded her brother. "I thought playing basketball was too hard, and I told the coach I can't do it. He said, 'Use persistence, keep practicing, and learn how to play a better game.' I did, and now I'm a member of the team. You can use persistence too. I know you can do your homework." He smiled at his sister before he walked on down the hall.

Just then Christine's mom came into the room and said, "I want to show you something."

"What is it?" Christine asked.

"Look what I have in my hand."

Christine stood up and walked over to take a closer look. "I see a necklace with beads of red stones. That's pretty," Christine said.

"Look closely at the stones," her mom suggested.

Christine bent over to get a closer look.

"Notice how the stones are cut and polished," her mom said.

"I see," Christine said.

"Each one was cut and polished by hand," her mom said.

"By hand? Do you mean someone made it?" Christine asked.

"Yes, a jeweler I know takes each rough stone, cuts and polishes it until it sparkles. Then he strings the stones into a necklace."

"That must take a long time to polish each stone," marveled Christine.

"Yes, the jeweler has the persistence to keep on working until the last stone is cut, polished, and made into a necklace.

"It sure is pretty."

Would you like to borrow it while you do your homework?"

"Oh, yes," responded Christine.

Her mom put the necklace around Christine's neck and fastened the clasp.

Christine looked at herself in her mirror. She smiled as she thought, *If a jeweler can cut and polish each stone, then I can have the persistence to correct my homework. I'll keep working until it is finished and beautiful.*

Christine walked back to her desk, picked up her pencil and corrected two spelling errors. *This is not as hard as I thought I would be. What's next?* She looked at her paper. *I'm supposed to add an adjective. I can add one.*

Christine continued editing her paper until she made all the corrections and additions. She put her pencil down, smiled and said to herself, *I have persistence.*

Persistence: Relaxation and Directions

RELAXATION: FOCUS ON YOUR BREATH

Be aware of your breath.

> *(pause)*

Feel your breath going in and out, in and out.

> *(pause)*

Notice how fast or slow your breath is going in and out, in and out.

> *(pause)*

Gently feel your breath going in and out, in and out.

> *(pause)*

DIRECTIONS

Choose a project or task you have completed in school or at home. When the music begins, remember how it felt to have the persistence to stay with the task until it was completed.

MUSIC

Play *Air on G string* from *Overture (Suite) No. 3 in D major*, BWV 106 by Bach.
4:57 minutes

At the end of the piece of music, softly say, "The music has ended. Gently bring your awareness back to this room."

SHARING

    1. Write about your experience.

        or

    2. Draw your experience.

        or

    3. Tell about your experience.

Possibilities

"I just don't know what to do. How will I ever finish this science project when I don't know where to start?" Julia complained. "It's due in three weeks and I don't know where to begin."

"You sound like you're afraid you won't find any ideas for your project," her mother said.

"I can't even think of one idea," Julia said, as she cupped her chin in her hands.

"Why don't you go for a walk in the woods? You might be inspired by something in nature," her mom suggested.

"That's a silly idea," Julia said. "Shouldn't I look in my science book?"

"Science is about nature. Go on a nature walk, and look at the possibilities that are all around you," her mother said.

"I guess that's better than just sitting here," Julia said, as she stood up and walked out the door. She paused as she felt the warm sun on her face.

She looked around. She was not the only one facing the sun. The sunflower plant at the side of the yard was facing the sun, and so were some of the flowers in the garden. Julia realized, flowers turn toward the light of the sun so they can grow. What is that big word? Ah, I remember, it's photosynthesis. I could do my project on photosynthesis and show how plants use light.

Julia walked through the garden. Something white and fluffy floated past her. Julia reached out to catch it. When she looked closely, she saw white strands attached to a tiny seed. *This seed can start a new milkweed plant,* she thought. *There must have been hundreds of seeds in the pod, and those seeds could grow hundreds of new plants.* She blew a milkweed seed off her hand and watched it float away in the breeze. *I could do my project on how seeds spread on the wind.*

Julia continued to walk through the garden. She noticed green beans on a vine, okra growing tall, and tomatoes growing bigger. *I wonder which ones my mom will pick for dinner. Hmm, I could do my project on gardening.*

Julia turned and walked toward the woods. "Ouch!" she said as she looked down. There was something sharp sticking to her sock. She carefully picked it off and saw prickles surrounding a seed. *The prickles stick on someone like me who will carry the seed to a new place. When it falls to the ground, it can grow into a new plant. Maybe other prickles from this plant are on the fur of my dog, or maybe a raccoon or maybe a . . . Oh, there are so many possibilities, I can't name them all. I could do my project on how prickly seeds travel on the bodies of other animals.*

Julia tossed the prickly seed into the woods. When it fell, she noticed the leaves on the ground. She took a stick and poked into the leaves to see what was below. A black bug scurried off; so did a centipede. *I bet there are earthworms under here.* She dug deeper, and sure enough, there were the worms. *If there are so many creatures here in one spot, how many are under the ground? I could do my project on creatures living under the ground.*

Julia stood up and heard the sound of *honk, honk, honk*. She looked up to the sky and saw birds in the shape of a 'V.' *They are Canada geese flying together. When they fly so high, they can see ponds and lakes below where they can get food and water. I could do my project on bird migration.*

Julia looked up when she heard the sound *pret-ty, pret-ty, pret-ty. That's the song of a cardinal.* She looked up in the tree and saw a red cardinal sitting on a branch and thought, *I'm glad you will stay here all winter. Your red feathers will look so pretty against the white snow when you visit our bird-feeder. Our seeds are just one possibility of food for you. You know how to find berries and seeds from the plants. I could do my project on what birds eat in the winter.*

Julia ran back to her house to tell her mom, "Now I have too many possibilities for my science project. I could choose how seeds spread on the wind, gardening, how prickly seeds travel on animals, creatures under the ground, bird migration, or what birds eat in winter. How do I choose from all of these possibilities?"

Her mom smiled and said, "It's a blessing to have so many possibilities. Choose any one your heart desires."

Possibilities: Relaxation and Directions

RELAXATION: STRETCHING

Stretch one leg.

(pause)

Now relax the muscles in that leg and notice how your leg feels.

(pause)

Stretch the other leg.

(pause)

Now relax the muscles in that leg and notice how your leg feels.

(pause)

Stretch one arm.

(pause)

Now relax the muscles in that arm and notice how your arm feels.

(pause)

Stretch your other arm.

(pause)

Now relax the muscles in that arm and notice how your arm feels.

(pause)

Stretch your spine from its base to where it joins your head.

(pause)

Now relax the muscles around your spine.

(pause)

Notice how long your spine is.

(pause)

DIRECTIONS

Choose a project or task you have to do. It could be a project in school, or job you have to do.

When the music begins, imagine possibilities of the various ways you could do your project or task.

MUSIC

Play *Le pas espagnol* from *Dolly Suite d'orchestre*, by Faure.
2:34 minutes

At the end of the piece of music, softly say, "The music has ended. Gently bring your awareness back to the classroom."

SHARING

1. Write about your experience.

    or

2. Draw your experience.

    or

3. Tell us about your experience.

Respect

Ken stood in front of the bulletin board and read the big word in bright red letters – R E S P E C T. He frowned and thought, *How can there be respect when "Gorilla Boy" is on the playground? He's mean, and I'm afraid he might hurt me.*

Ken turned away from the bulletin board and walked down the hall toward his classroom. Suddenly he heard the words, "Get out of my way!" Ken's hair felt like it was standing straight up like a fur on a scared cat.

"Hey, 'Pumpkin Head', get out of my way."

Ken moved as quickly he could toward the wall and pressed his back against the wall.

Gorilla Boy stomped down the hall. Ken looked at his broad shoulders and muscular body and thought, *I don't want to mess with him.*

"Why are you standing with your back against the wall?" Dave asked as he passed Ken. "Come on, we don't want to be late for class."

Ken walked fast to catch up with his friend. When they walked into class the teacher said, "Today we will explore the word respect. What is respect?"

Cynthia raised her hand and said, "Respect is when my brother has time to help me with my math homework."

The teacher nodded and asked, "How do you feel when he helps you?"

Stories, Music, and Imagery Process

"I feel like he cares about me."

Tommy raised his hand to say, "I showed respect when I held the door for the next person when we walked out of the store."

The teacher nodded and said, "You didn't even know that person, and you showed that you were considerate."

Barbara said, "I showed respect for myself by going to bed early when I was tired."

The class laughed, and the teacher said, "Respecting others begins with respect for yourself. When you respect yourself, then you can respect another person.

"Look at this rhyme," continued the teacher, as she pointed to board in the front of the classroom. "Listen to its rhythm as I read it."

R-E-S-P-E-C-T

It's not just a word it's a way to be.

Thoughtful, caring, and considerate.

And I start by respecting me.

"Your assignment is to write about a time when you respected yourself, and two times when you respected someone else."

Ken took out his pencil and paper and began to write down the rhyme. He read the words, felt the rhythm, and started to tap the rhythm of the words.

When did I have respect for me, Ken wondered. *I know, I didn't wait until the last minute to do my homework project. I did a little each day until it was completed. I didn't have to panic the day before it was due.*

Where else was I respectful? I saw Gail's pen ran out of ink. I had an extra pen and handed it to her. I liked the way she smiled. There, I have two examples of respect. Now I need just one more.

"It's the end of class," announced the teacher. "Finish writing your three examples of respect and bring what you wrote to class tomorrow."

Ken put his paper into his backpack and walked out the door toward the carpool line. "Oops," he said. "I forgot my lunchbox." He went back to get it.

When he came out of his room, no one else was in the hall except for . . . . "Gorilla Boy."

Ken took a deep breath and started to hum the respect rhyme in his head. He didn't realize it, but he was tapping the rhythm on his book bag with his fingers. "Gorilla Boy" walked past him and paused to look his fingers tapping the rhythm.

Ken realized he was tapping and humming, and said, "This is the rhythm of the respect rhyme we learned in class."

"Gorilla Boy" said, "Here is a cool rhythm I heard on the radio." He began tapping and mouthing the rhythm.

Ken smiled. "Gorilla Boy" nodded, then continued down the hallway.

"Goodbye George," Ken said as he realized, *this is the first time I called him by his name.*

Ken walked toward carpool line and thought, *This is my third example. I shared my respect rhythm with someone who is scary, and I was not afraid.*

Ken continued tapping his respect rhythm all the way to the carpool line.

Respect: Relaxation and Directions

RELAXATION: LETTING GO OF TENSION

Allow your breath to become slow and steady.

(pause)

Notice a place in your body where there is tension or tightness.

(pause)

Breathe into that tense place.

(pause)

The next time you exhale, let go of some of that tightness.

(pause)

Each time you exhale, let go of more tightness.

(pause)

When that place in your body feels relaxed and comfortable, find another place in your body where there is tension or tightness.

(pause)

Breathe into that tense place, and let go of the tension.

(pause)

DIRECTIONS

Let the music help you remember a time when you respected yourself and two other people. Notice what you feel. Notice your thoughts.

MUSIC

Play *Minuet L'Arlesienne Suite No. 2* by Bizet.
4:05 minutes

At the end of the piece of music, softly say, "The music has ended. Gently bring your awareness back to this room."

SHARING

1. Write about your experience.

    or

2. Draw your experience.

    or

3. Tell about your experience.

About the Author

Linda T. Powell taught music in public and private schools for over thirty years. While teaching in the Atlanta Public Schools, she created and implemented a program using music and imagery to encourage children to grow their self-worth. *Stories, Music, and Imagery: A Doorway to a Child's Self-Esteem* is being used by teachers, parents, and counselors, and is available on Kindle and Apple.

Her second book, *Character Education Through Stories, Music, and Imagery,* includes twenty original stories and clear directions for how to use this process with children. This book can support character education programs in schools, and be used by teachers, parents, and counselors to encourage children to recognize and grow their heart qualities.

Linda completed her three-year training program in The Bonny Method of Guided Imagery and Music (GIM), obtained her Orff music Level Certification from Memphis State, Master of Music Degree from the University of Michigan, and Bachelor of Music Education degree from Boston University.

Linda teaches at the Adawehi Healing Center in Columbus, NC, and uses music and imagery with children and teens to help them discover their inner wisdom. She enjoys teaching Orff music classes, drumming, and piano lessons.

About the Illustrator

June Ellen Bradley is an artist, naturalist, and environmental educator. Moreover, June Ellen is a senior mentor at the Green River Preserve in Cedar Mountain, NC.

She trained with Tom Brown at the Tracker School, Inc. and has a BA in Biology and Government from Wheaton College, Norton, MA.

June Ellen puts her heart into her art. Can you find a little heart in all the drawings in this book? Look for the little heart in each of the illustrations.

June Ellen Bradley can be reached through JuneEllenBradley.com.